CARING & COMMITMENT

CARING

&

COMMITMENT

Learning to Live the Love We Promise

Lewis B. Smedes

1817

Harper & Row, Publishers, San Francisco
Cambridge, Hagerstown, New York, Philadelphia, Washington
London, Mexico City, São Paulo, Singapore, Sydney

In Grateful Memory

of

RENA BENEDICTUS SMEDES

Keeper of Commitment

FIRST EDITION

Library of Congress Catalog Card Number: 87-45723
ISBN: 0-06-067418-0

Contents

For People Who Believe in Commitment... and Wonder Why

I wonder what our lives would be like if this were the most we could ever get from anyone: "I'll be there if I can, but don't count on it."

We would go crazy, wouldn't we, if we could *never* count on anybody to make a promise to us and keep it. We would go insane with uncertainty if none of the people we need to trust the most—our wives, our husbands, our friends, our parents—ever made and kept a commitment.

But I wonder what life would be like if we were stuck forever to every commitment we ever made. Absolutely stuck! So that we were never allowed to cut our losses and start over after a bad beginning.

Life would be cruel, wouldn't it? If we could never get a release from bad commitments? We would all be prisoners of our past mistakes, padlocked into promises we made when we didn't truly know what we were promising.

Our deepest relationships are held together by an invisible cord called commitment. Every important community we have with other people depends on the strength of that unseen cord. If we don't dare to make commitments or don't care enough to keep them, we destabilize the relationships that most need to be steady and we leave the people who most need to count on us unsure of where they stand. The fact is that we can keep our lives together only if we can trust each other to make and keep commitments.

On the other hand, if we are *never* free to start over again, we condemn some people to a slow death.

I am awestruck by how much we need commitment from each other. But I am impressed too with how impossible it is, sometimes, to keep the commitments we have made.

To find our way between the craziness of life without commitment and the cruelty of bondage to all past commitments— this is my reason for writing this book.

In 1985 distinguished University of California sociologist Robert Bellah and four of his colleagues published an important study about the loss of commitment in American life. *Habits of the Heart* they called it, and gave it the subtitle *Individualism and Commitment in American Life*. Bellah's group came to the conclusion that most of us don't really believe in commitment anymore. We believe instead in every individual's right to pursue his or her own fulfillment. And since we believe most in our own right to be satisfied with life, we shy from commitments that could tie us to people who lack the power to bring us the satisfaction to which we feel entitled.

My own experience gives me a different point of view. Most people I know do believe in commitment; they do want genuinely committed relationships with others. But they are not always sure what a commitment asks of them. Or what they should do when a commitment that they once made, and made sincerely, becomes very painful, maybe impossible, to keep.

The people I know best are not human butterflies. They don't flutter through other people's lives, stopping long enough to get what they want out of them, and then flying off. They don't live with their bags packed, moving on whenever the grass looks greener down the street, leaving somebody else to pick up the pieces. No, I am writing for people who really do believe in commitment.

But they sometimes find that the road of commitment keeping is rough, and the arguments for calling it quits are powerful.

If you are the sort of person who believes in commitment, but wonders sometimes what your commitment really asks of you when you get into the hard places, I wrote this book for you. I invite you to join me on a small adventure into the many risky relationships of life that depend on people who dare to make and care to keep commitments.

Before we get going, though, I need to tell you about the kind of commitments we will be exploring.

I will be talking only about commitments to *people*. To narrow it down a little more, I will be talking about commitments we make to our friends, commitments we as parents make to our children, and, especially, commitments we make to our husbands and wives. I will also talk about commitments we make to ourselves.

These are the sorts of commitments we need to renew over and over again in the countless small choices we make from day to day, sometimes hour to hour. And the sorts of commitments that a person *can* walk away from whenever he or she takes a notion. We are not stuck to them by some natural instinct or force of necessity. We are free not to keep any commitment. It's up to us.

This book is about the personal risks we take when we do make commitments, and about the struggles we often have in keeping them. It's about discovering the way to make love last through the winter seasons of life. Should you choose to go with me on this adventure, we will walk together on the path of one of life's most amazing graces—the gift of promised love.

Part 1

THE CELEBRATION OF COMMITMENT

CHAPTER 1

The High Stakes of Commitment

I make an appointment with someone, with you, perhaps, for sometime in any of your tomorrows, and all the future tomorrows that follow your yesterdays.

I reach out into a future that neither of us can see, and I plan a meeting with you, and ask you to trust me to be there with you.

I stretch myself into unpredictable days ahead and make one thing predictable for you: I will be there with you.

I create a small island of certainty for you in the swirling waters of our uncertainties: it is the certainty of my presence with you.

I make space in my life for you that you know will be there waiting for you, even if every other place is crowded.

These are some of the things I do when I make a commitment to another human being.

How strange it is, when you think about it, that a mere human being can take hold of the future and fasten one part of it down for another person. That ordinary people can lift their lives a good notch above their whims and their impulses and their desires, and secure their lives together in the face of all the fretful fates that lie in waiting. How wonderful it is that we can offer each other one mooring as we face our free-floating futures— the mooring of trust in each other's commitments.

We have a mystery on our hands, no doubt about it: it is the mystery of how we, weak and limited persons that we are, can look all the uncertainty of life full in the face and say, I will make one thing certain: my presence in the life of another person.

The mystery gets deeper when we consider that there are

always two essential ingredients to a personal commitment. Two components. And we need both of them equally.

A personal commitment is a blend of *consistency* and *care*.

Let's take *consistency* first.

The *Los Angeles Times* has a nifty slogan: "We are there for you every day." And they are. They have been there for me at my address every morning for more than fifteen years. It is nice to know that come flood, hail, or desert sun, I can count on waking up to the plop of the *Los Angeles Times* on my driveway.

I have never seen the person who brings me the *Los Angeles Times* at the break of every dawn: he has never stopped on his rounds to ring my doorbell and ask me how things are going with the folks in my house. I don't know whether he cares a fig about me, or about any of the people at whose homes he delivers the paper every morning. And I don't mind. All I really want from him is consistency—the paper, same time, every day.

But this is not commitment: his consistency is only a matter of contract, of giving me that for which I pay.

When it comes to a commitment between two persons, we need *care* as well as consistency.

When I care about you, I deliver my*self* to you. Which is a lot different from delivering a newspaper every morning. Consistency has to do with *predictability*. Caring has to do with *personal presence*. The people who deliver the *Los Angeles Times* are predictable, that is, they deliver the paper to me consistently. My wife brings her very self to me in caring love; she is present as well as predictable.

It isn't enough to be predictable. Not in personal commitments. But it isn't enough to be present either.

I have an acquaintance who is powerfully present with me when he is there. He looks me in the eye when he talks to me, pays attention to everything I say, makes me feel as if I am the only thing of importance in his life at that moment. He makes me believe that he cares. And when he leaves he promises to call me, and he says, "We'll have lunch."

But he doesn't call, and he doesn't return my calls. We don't have lunch. I don't see him again until we happen to meet at a party. And I feel let down. I need consistency as well as care.

Presence without predictability, care without consistency: it's not enough. Any more than consistency without care is enough. Commitment is both.

But all this only raises the stakes and increases the risk. We promise so much of ourselves when we know so little about what things are going to be like when the time comes to keep the commitments we make. Consider the risk.

WE WILL CHANGE

I won't be quite the same person tomorrow that I am today. I will change. My needs will change. My desires will change. So will my feelings.

When I promise to be with you, I do not know for sure what I will be like at some distant time when you will need me. Yet I expect that the person I will become will keep the commitment that I make today.

You will change as much as I will. I do not know what you will be like in some distant tomorrow. Will you be attractive? Healthy? Will you change your mind about the important things we both believe in now? Will you feel differently about me? Will you want me to be near you? How can I know for sure?

Yet I expect to keep my commitment to you, whoever you turn out to be in the future.

Circumstances will change too. Neither of us knows what life will be like when the time comes for us to keep the commitment we make today. Will times be hard? Will other people have come into your life to crowd me out? Will life be too difficult for us to manage together? How can we know?

And yet I expect to keep my commitment to you in the future, however tough the times.

A commitment has a "no matter what" quality about it. No matter how I change. No matter what happens to you. No matter what happens around us. It has the feel of *unconditionality*.

What a risk!

And how high the stakes!

The stakes are high for us because we surrender so much when we make serious commitments to people. We stand to gain a lot too: maybe love, maybe life. But let's not discount the surrender.

There are at least three things we surrender when we commit ourselves to another person.

We surrender our *freedom.*

We surrender our *individuality.*

We surrender our *control.*

All in all, a lot of surrender. Before we go on, we had better take a good look at each of them just to make sure we know beforehand how much we surrender.

WE SURRENDER OUR FREEDOM

When we make a commitment, we freely decide that our lives will not flow free, unattached, from one personal relationship to another. We set our minds—in advance—to say no to some offers that come our way. Our commitment builds an invisible fence around us, and we freely choose to respect the limits.

WE SURRENDER OUR INDIVIDUALITY

When we commit ourself to someone else, we stretch beyond our individual self and put ourself at the side of another. I put myself beside you, to walk with you into the heather of the hidden hills before us. Once committed, I am no longer a separate *I.* The mirror of myself no longer shows a solitary being, standing alone, by himself, an isolated individual. I am plural, one of us; my unity is we.

Who am I? I am who I am in linkage with you; you are part of my definition.

WE SURRENDER OUR CONTROL

When we commit ourself to another, we give up control over a segment of our own life. For we let another person stake a claim on ourself. The person to whom we make a commitment can call us back to himself or herself with two simple words: You promised. And we give up our right to say; I don't care. So somebody else shares control with me, control over my own life.

All in all, it's a lot to surrender, and done in the sure knowledge that we are going to change. Yet we make our commitment. High risk. With a lot at stake.

This brings me to the most critical point of all. *The only way to live with the high risk of commitment is trust.*

When I commit myself to you, I expect you to trust me. You

know that I am capable of leaving you. You know that I can let you down. So I make my commitment and expect you to trust me to keep it.

But then I need to trust you too. I have to trust you not to abuse my commitment, not to scorn it, not to deflate it. I trust that you will not turn me away when I want to be present with you. I trust you to treat my commitment kindly.

Trust is our only guarantee. But this is not a guarantee at all, not in the sense of a sure thing backed by a contract that can hold up in court. We can draw up a contract between us, and my contract may limit your losses if I should leave you, or mine if you should leave me. But no contract can tell us for sure that I will stay with you, or you with me, when staying costs us something.

Our trust is not blind; our inner eye, our heart, has its own way of seeing. We trust because our inner eye sees each other's sincerity and character. What we see reduces the risk. It does not ensure against pain—not the way Lloyds of London can insure against disaster. But it offers us the peculiar kind of hope that dares to take the high risk of personal commitment. Without trust, nobody in his or her right mind would ever make a serious commitment to another person. With trust, a person dares to gamble on a lasting partnership of caring love.

To summarize: a personal commitment is one of life's high risk adventures. For when we commit ourselves to people, we look into a future that is not going to be quite like the present, and we promise that we will be there, truly present, consistently and caringly, with people who may not be able to give us all we had expected from them. And the way we will make our commitment work is not by contract, not by force, but by the risky personal gift of trust.

CHAPTER 2

The Real Reasons People Keep Commitments

Let's admit, to begin with, that not everyone who sticks with a relationship stays out of loyalty to a commitment.

Some people are just covering their bets. They have too much to lose by separating. So they choose the lesser of two evils, and stick it out.

Some people just get used to each other. They don't like surprises; they stay with each other because they feel settled in. Comfortable.

She knows when he's coming home, what he will say when he gets in the door, what he drinks before supper and what he is likely to talk about while he eats dinner, how he takes his clothes off—shoes first, shirt next, then socks, and when he is likely to get a notion to make love. He never unsettles her with the shocker that he has changed his mind. She knows what he is going to say, he knows what she is going to say, so mostly, neither bothers.

Oh, one could get cynical about such "commitments." The jaded confessor in the Albert Camus book *The Fall* looked at one man's commitment this way: "I knew a man who gave twenty years of his life to a scatterbrained woman, sacrificing everything to her, his friendships, his work, the very respectability of his life, and who one evening recognized that he had never loved her. He had been bored, that's all, bored like most people . . . *and that explains most human commitments* . . . Hurrah then for funerals."

Let the cynic have his say. I put his misanthropic sentiments on record, just to show that there is more than one way to look at some commitments.

But why grouse about settledness? What looks like soul-choking boredom to people who prefer not to know what's coming next, can be gentle settledness for those of us who do better without daily surprises. And settledness wears well. Even if it doesn't keep the joy bells clanging in our hearts.

Other people stay around because they wager that what they have is not as bad as what they think may be the alternative.

There could be a badgered banker in Sioux Falls who would leave his wife tomorrow if he did not put such a high price tag on his place in the community. He has a severe case of the twenty-year itch, and is absolutely certain that a life-satisfying relationship—to which he feels he has every right—is waiting for him just beyond the boundaries of the marriage that throttles his untested potential for passion. But he, being prudent as well as itchy, knows he needs the respect of all the folk at First Reformed Church; he can't afford to get out of good graces with the profamily constituency there. He needs the goodwill of his wife's family also; it owns too big a chunk of Sioux Falls real estate, hefty collateral on bank loans, for him to risk alienation from them. And he wants to keep his old friends. So he sticks with his marriage, mainly because he is so heavily invested in Sioux Falls.

Transplant the Sioux Falls banker to Southern California, give him big city anonymity, where he could be divorced several times over without anyone at First National headquarters even noticing, and he might leave his wife two months after arrival. But at First National of Sioux Falls, he has to be the very model of marital reliability.

Credit the banker with common sense, but don't give him an A+ for commitment.

Other people are simply trapped. A talented lady I know has agoraphobia, a fear of open spaces—and a husband who brutalizes her in several subtle styles. I think she would leave in a minute, but she can't get away because she does not dare go outside to look for a job and she can't afford to live anywhere else but at home with him.

Give her credit, maybe, for not putting arsenic in his coffee, but don't confuse her staying with commitment.

Not everybody sticks with what he or she is stuck with out of a heroic effort to keep a promise. I mean no discredit. It's simply that many of us stick with things because the alternatives to staying are even less attractive.

But let's talk about people who really do choose to live by promises—spoken or unspoken—they have made. They don't keep their promises simply because they have made them once and are stuck with them. In fact, commitment keepers don't usually think much about the fact that they have made promises.

They don't stay because they feel stuck to a vow that some eternal law obliges them to keep; they just care about the persons to whom they are quietly committed.

This came to me one afternoon while I was visiting my mother in her private room at the osteopathic hospital in Muskegon, Michigan, where she was secretly getting ready to die, at age eighty-six, not having the ginger anymore to face another round of learning how to take painful baby steps with a semi-repaired hip. I, having come to Michigan for a week's worth of morning workshops, was just a half hour's drive away, with my afternoons free for long talks with her. As it turned out, this was our last visit together; she took her leave, pretty much as she decided, a couple of weeks after I left.

My mother, I must tell you, left her farm home in Friesland, that rambunctious province of northernmost Netherlands where they still speak their own ancient Frisian tongue, came to Western Michigan at age twenty with a dreamer of a Frisian husband, to pursue the American dream. Her husband, my father, stayed with her for eleven years, long enough to bring five children and no money into the home, and then, at age thirty-two, died and went to heaven, leaving her on earth with us five kids but with hardly five dollars to put shoes on our feet. She was just thirty-one, a lonely young beauty, with no money, no social security, no relatives, no job skills, and only a very loose hold on the English language.

It was tough going for her. But she did it, her way, the best she could manage, which was fine on the whole. She never made a move to find another man and, as far as I can remember, she never talked about the possibility. As I got older, though, I wondered about this part of her life. Did this woman, this needy woman, this passionate, lonely person, never long for a male in her life, never yearn for a man to sleep with, to make love with, a strong man to help her carry her load?

So I asked her, I barged into her heart's private place where honor used to close the door to nosy sons. "Mother, you were a good-looking woman, and you must have been terribly lonely. You had a right to some happiness. Didn't you ever want a man, someone who would take care of you, love you, marry you?"

She answered as if she had been wondering why it had taken us all so long to ask. "Yes," she said, "I wanted a man, and I thought about getting married again if someone would have me, but I was afraid that if I took a man into the house, he might not love my children, and I cared too much for them to take the risk."

I'm sorry that she never felt the strong love of a man after my father died. I am not writing this to say that she did the best thing. I mention it only as a witness to her reason for keeping a commitment against the claims of her own deep and natural desires. Keeping her commitment really was nothing more than a way of caring for us, the way we were, there, in front of her nose, pains in the neck that we often were.

She did not need moral prodding from the memory of a promise. And she created her commitment again each day out of everyday's relentless choices. She chose every day anew to slug it out with a secondhand washing machine that broke down every other Monday as she washed other people's clothes. She renewed her commitment every morning that she hustled out to scrub somebody's floors as soon as she could get us kids off to school. She recommitted herself every time one of us got into trouble with the neighbors or came down with scarlet fever. She was forever making routine choices that kept her commitment alive. And by these small choices she was telling us that she would be there with us when the foundations of our little corner of the earth shook.

She was committed, heaven knows. But she was committed *without thinking* about being committed. She knew nothing about "commitment," she only knew she cared.

Another reason we keep commitments has to do with *belonging* to people.

Belonging to people is risky. It could be a subtle way of being owned by somebody, the way a person can own a hunk of real estate, a chattel, or a slave. But we can also belong to people simply by putting ourselves at their side. Their place becomes our place. Their needs become our needs. Their destiny our destiny. Belonging can be a way of loving.

The Albert Camus story *The Plague* is about a person's sense of belonging and therefore about commitment, even though nobody mentions the word.

The people of the town of Oran knew they were in for something dreadful when the rats came out of the dark places to die in their streets and hallways and when, once the rats were all dead, the citizens began to die the same way. The cup of dread was full by the time a thousand persons were dying of the plague every week, and the sanitation department began hauling bodies by the tramload, at night, when nobody was looking, to a city dump. Eventually the town was quarantined to protect other towns in the province; nobody could get in or out.

Dr. Bernard Rieux was caught in the plague, just like everyone else, and it never occurred to him to try to get out of town, even though he longed to join his wife, who happened at the time to be a patient at a resort in the country.

A journalist named Raymond Rambert was caught in Oran too, and he wanted to get out in the worst way. "Why should I stay," he asked Dr. Rieux, "I'm different from the rest of the people; I don't belong here."

But he was stuck. And, for nothing better to do, he began going with Dr. Rieux on his daily rounds to make dying a little less horrible for the people, and maybe save some children. Rambert pitched in, doing whatever a layperson could do to help people die with some dignity.

One day a person smuggler offered Rambert a chance to get out—for a price.

But he surprised Rieux by deciding to stay.

Stay? Why stay, Rieux asked. "Your happiness is waiting for you in Paris. You have every *right* to be happy. And you certainly cannot be happy here."

Rambert's answer provides us with one of the better secrets of why people keep commitments: "Until now I always felt a stranger in this town, and that I'd no concern with you people. But now that I've seen what I have seen, I know that I *belong* here whether I want it or not."

Rambert and Rieux were in the same boat; they were committed because they belonged.

Other people keep commitments because they feel as if they were born into a new identity when they made a commitment.

John Cooper is a good example. John married a sturdy, spritely woman named Margie back in 1941 and settled in with Margie in high hopes of becoming the country's biggest onion grower. But four years later, after bearing him two children who were just then mightily in need of caring for, Margie fell victim to polio. She spent the rest of her life in an iron lung.

Gone were the payoffs John had expected from his alliance with Margie. No housekeeper, no sex partner, no childbearer, no budget balancer. Gone too was the high hope of a big onion farm; you can't compete in big league onion farming when you are spending chunks of every day taking care of a wife who has polio.

John and Margie Cooper had a fortieth wedding anniversary a few years ago, and someone who didn't know John well asked him to explain his long devotion. "I'm a Christian," he said, "and we try to keep our promises." But it was not as if he would have ditched Margie years ago had his morality not stuck him to a vow he had made.

To people like John, a promise is like being born. John Cooper did the same thing a person born with a handicap does; he accepted his and Margie's situation as a condition of the life he was born into when he made his commitment to her.

When Margie died, their son Dale asked John how he had done what he had done all those years. "I never even thought about doing anything else. You just do it, and God helps you."

You just do it. But only if you let your significant commitments be a kind of birth into a new dimension of your reality.

Sometimes, though, when the whole thing seems to be falling apart, when a person has a lot of good reasons to move on, that person may be reminded that one day, ten years or a lifetime ago, he or she made a promise. It is as simple as that.

This is how Maggie Antrobus feels about it. There is a terrible struggle going on between her and George Antrobus, her husband of who knows how many years. Oh, make no mistake,

George is a fine man; he made his way up from almost nothing, he's been an excellent father, a pillar of the church, and has all the best interests of the community at heart. And Maggie is as fine a woman as you could hope to meet. She lives for her children, is, in fact, the acting president of the Excelsior Mother's Club, and does needlecraft so well that people want her to go into business.

Maggie and George are old, thousands of years old, to be truthful; they are the central characters in Thornton Wilder's 1940s play *The Skin of Our Teeth.*

There has been a war. Strange things have happened to George during the upheaval. For one thing, he has fallen in love with a another woman and, as we meet him, he is about to leave Maggie, once and for all, and make his bid for happiness.

GEORGE: "Maggie, I'm moving out . . . of everything. For good. I'm going to marry Miss Fairweather. I shall provide generously for you and the children. In a few years you'll be able to see that it's all for the best. That's all I have to say. . . . You're a fine woman, Maggie, but . . . but a man has his own life to lead in the world."

MAGGIE: "Well, after living with you for five thousand years I guess I have a right to a word or two, haven't I?' "

GEORGE: "I want to spare your feelings in every way I can, Maggie."

MAGGIE: calmly, almost dreamily; "I didn't marry you because you were perfect. I didn't even marry you because I loved you. I married you because you gave me a promise. . . . That promise made up for your faults. And the promise I gave you made up for mine. Two imperfect people got married and it was the promise that made the marriage."

GEORGE: "Maggie . . . I was only nineteen."

MAGGIE: "And when our children were growing up, it wasn't a house that protected them; and it wasn't our love that protected them—it was that promise."

But the war changed the way George felt about things: "When you're at war you think about a better life; when you're at peace you think about a more comfortable life. I've lost it."

"Oh, George, you have to get it back again. Think! What else kept us alive all these years? Even now, it's not comfort we want. We can suffer whatever's necessary; only give us back that promise."

George does begin to wake up to what really keeps life together: "Oh, I've never forgotten for long at a time that living is a struggle. I know that every good and excellent thing in the world stands moment by moment on the razor edge of danger, and must be fought for. . . . Maggie, we've come a long way. We've learned. We're learning. And the steps of our journey are marked for us here."

He gave her back the promise.

The future is possible, sometimes, only because people remember a promise of the past. And keep it. Walk with their promise into tomorrow with some hope that, even if things are not perfect for them, their life together will be better than tolerable, probably even good, and maybe just fine.

Let's see, before going on, if we can squeeze the essence out this chapter. People sometimes stick with people only because they can't get away; this is not what I mean by commitment, though I'm not making light of it. Genuine commitment means that they stay with each other because they *care* enough about each other to stay.

They stay because they finally get to feeling that they *belong* to each other.

They stay because they simply *accept the conditions of the life they were born into* when they made their commitment.

And, they sometimes stay because *they promised they would*.

And, all in all, these are not bad reasons for keeping a commitment.

CHAPTER 3

The Positive Purpose Behind Personal Commitments

The truth is that Peter was not all that brilliant, and he probably would not have made it at medical school if Eloise hadn't nagged him through his endless exams while she earned rent and grocery money doing night duty as a nurse in the intensive care unit at Butterworth Hospital.

He and Eloise had some good times and some bad times together since Peter started practicing internal medicine ten years ago at a total care clinic in Amherst, Massachusetts. The best times, for Eloise, were the August weeks they spent at her father's cabin off the coast of southern Maine. The worst times were when she was pregnant, always very sick, not much fun to be with, and during which Peter would devote his spare time to a meaningful personal relationship he was cultivating, nothing sexual, mind you, but still fairly intimate, with a handsome Amherst woman who was under his tender care for a chronic backache. In between the best and worst times were the times of muddling through the bringing up of two boys, refining their tennis serves, all while Peter needled his narrow way into a lucrative pocket of the well-paid medical fraternity of well-kept Amherst.

But then Peter actually fell in love, a freefall into the affections of one of those gifted women who get more exciting as they get older, a late bloomer, and a survivor who had entered law school at thirty-five after her divorce—mostly to prove to her ex-husband that she was more than equal to him—and had found herself in no time at all making a lot of money writing up trusts for rich folks trying to preserve their legacies. Endowed with a strong mouth, narrow nose, and long legs, she strode around in her Burberry coat and scarf, as if she were always just on time for an important appointment. But she never seemed hassled. Not one to be indirect, blunt may be the word, she let Peter know soon enough that what she wanted from him was a very close relationship. Stunned that an elegant woman like her was attracted to him, Peter fell in love, and out of commitment.

Eloise agreed a little too quickly with Peter that the blossom of their love had wilted into mutual toleration. She had gotten frumpy, she knew it, her intellectual curiosity had never been feverish, and the erotic current that in days almost forgotten had flown through their connected circuits had turned itself off during her second pregnancy. The apparent stability of their marriage was really a frayed blanket hiding Peter's nagging boredom.

But when Peter told her he wanted to leave and dared to ask for her blessing, he finally raised Eloise's dander.

"My blessing? You and that woman will burn in hell before you get my blessing, Peter. You *made a commitment* to me. You may get your middle-aged kicks from this snotty Amherst witch, but you are committed to *me*. Doesn't commitment mean anything to you, Peter?"

"Commitment? You talk commitment when my happiness is at stake? Our happiness is a lot more important than sticking to a lousy commitment we made a lifetime ago. Give me one good reason why I should be stuck with it now, just when I finally have something good going for me?"

"Why? Why? Just because you made it. That's why."

Is that why we keep commitments? Just because we made them?

It's not enough reason for my self-maximizer.

Having spilled the beans, I'll have to tell you more about my self-maximizer. He is the go-getter inside of me who tells me that my first job in life is to realize my potential. I have a simmering potful of uncooked potential within me, and my self-maximizer believes that I have a right, maybe a duty, to bring it to a boil.

My self-maximizer is the part of me that whispers exciting things to me about my untested capacity to feel things I have never felt, experience things I have never experienced, become things I have only dreamt about becoming.

He hints that commitment keeping is a sucker's game—a moral scam to cheat people such as Peter and me out of their last chance for happiness. He tells me that I might be a lot better off if I kept myself free to cut bait and move on if I wasn't catching my legal limit of satisfaction.

When his twin, the commitment keeper inside of me, reminds me that I have promises to keep, my self-maximizer suavely nudges me to invoke the bottom line of happiness: why should I let a mere commitment stand in the way of my inalienable right to the pursuit of total fulfillment?

So, having admitted that my own private self-maximizer tends to take Peter's point of view, I will consider Peter's question as if it were my own: why should Peter, or I, or you, put commitment keeping ahead of the pursuit of happiness?

Let's get rid of one bad answer first. I mean the answer that might go like this: we should keep commitments simply because people who keep their commitments are better people than those who don't.

The virtue of commitment keeping is not its own reward.

I grant that fidelity is an attractive quality in a person. We used to call it a *virtue*—which means it is one of the qualities we look for in first-rate people. Being a staunch person, a person of fealty, a loyal person, is to have the mark of excellence on you. Staying with sinking ships and losing causes, this is the stuff of virtue. Agreed. But, contrary to pious opinion, virtue is seldom its own reward, and the virtue of commitment keeping never is.

Becoming jut-jawed persons who preen themselves on their moral luster is not the reward we get for sticking to commitments. The reward for commitment keeping is a better kind of life for people who care about each other.

Some people sweat and snort through daily workouts so that they will be fit enough to sweat and snort through the workouts. "Why do you jog?" I asked my perspiring friend. "To keep fit," he answered. "And why do you want to keep fit?" I asked. "So that I can be in shape to jog," he replied. Good enough reason for fanatics, I suppose.

But surely we are not bound to commitments so that we can get in shape to keep our commitments. So that, in turn, we can look good to the connoisseurs of virtue.

I know of a man who makes a major moral production of his commitment keeping. He expects his grateful family to praise him with a morning hymn, "Great is Thy Faithfulness," at every breakfast time.

Everybody in town knows him for his moral character. He gets a loan from the bank, anytime, without collateral, on his reputation as a commitment keeper. Good old dependable Joe.

He reminds Janine, his wife, of his selfless devotion to their marriage, reminds her constantly; it always gives him an advantage. His voice slides into the nasal register, bordering on a sneer, as he reminds her of how he has never given her reason to doubt his fidelity, though, who knows, he has had chances enough.

He lets her know that he sticks around, not because she is worth sticking to, but because he is such a loyal character. So when he struts his commitment-keeping stuff, he ends up leaving Janine feeling like an unwanted woman who is cleaved to only because her husband is too moral to leave her.

Something almost always goes wrong when we keep our commitments out of commitment to our own commitment keeping. French novelist François Mauriac tells a story about someone he had the inspiration to call *The Woman of the Pharisees*. This woman, the *grande dame* of the valley, very rich in houses and land, was committed to the poor people in her village, visiting them all regularly, always leaving behind a gift suitable to their needs—as she saw them—along with a suggestion that a little more ambition and a little more thrift could improve their situation. She never left a poor family's house without making them feel worse for her having been there.

She flogged them with her commitment to them. And they hated her for the gifts almost as much as they hated themselves for accepting them. What she was committed to was her reputation as a rich woman committed to poor people.

Mauriac's story reminds me of an epitaph written by C. S. Lewis:

Erected by her sorrowing brothers
In memory of Martha Clay.
Here lies one who lived for others.
Now she has peace. And so have they.

In sum, getting to be virtuous is not reason enough to persuade us that commitment keeping is a rung or two higher on the ladder of life's duties than looking out for our own happiness.

What makes commitment keeping worth working at is this: it serves the long term good of people in relationship, people who want to live in a caring human community. That's the beginning and the end of it. We can create a good life together only out of trust. And trust, to make it last, needs commitment.

We need to know that people who promise to be with us are really going to be there. If we all lived as strictly free-floating, unfettered, self-enhancing individuals, we would all be left hanging in the vacuum of each other's undependability. We need something firmer.

Commitments give it to us. They create small islands of security for us in our oceans of insecurity. They make enclaves of steadiness in the jungles of change. They give us the only human basis for trusting each other. For counting on each other.

Commitment is the invisible fiber that binds a collection of individuals into a caring community. A large one or a small one. Everything depends on it. Everything from a family reunion to a concord of nations, from calling a committee meeting to founding a nation, from celebrating high mass to getting a return trip ticket to Pasadena. Not to mention a lasting marriage. Or a good friendship.

Maybe you can have a regime, or a gang, or a crowd, or a prison full of inmates, or even a foreign legion, without commitment, but you cannot have a human community. The only way we can, anywhere, anytime, create a good human relationship within a caring community is by daring to make and caring to keep commitments to each other.

So my answer to Peter's question—why should I stay with a commitment when happiness calls me away?—is the answer I give to my own self-maximizer: the reason for keeping our commitments to each other is that, in the long run, keeping commitments is the only way to have a community, and—as T. S.

Eliot reminded us—there is no human life that is not lived in human community.

Let me sum up: the right kind of commitment keeping makes good sense because it is the only way to keep good human relationships alive. And good human relationships make everybody's life better.

Commitments are worth the effort and, sometimes, the sacrifice, because, when all is said and done, people are almost always better off because of them. If we keep them the way they are meant to be kept—with care as well as with consistency— we are laying the foundation for the only kind of life fit for human beings. This is ultimately why commitment keeping is worth a try.

When my persistent self-maximizer asks for one single and sound reason *why* I should keep my commitments even more than I should maximize myself, I tell him what I have told you: it is better for us, and it makes life better for other people, if we make and keep commitments to each other. But there are more reasons than this. And we have to see how it works out in the fire and smoke of real life, where people are not always able to keep the commitments they have made.

CHAPTER 4

The Only Way to Make Love Last

I once thought of James Ettison as a not-very-profound person, but it was ungenerous of me to think of him that way. James was a salesman, on the road a good deal, and I think I envied him a little when a gentle and lovely woman I liked a lot fell in love with him. Her name was Alice, and he was as sure as a human being could be about anything that she would bring him all of his deepest desires.

They got married, and settled snugly, maybe smugly, into happiness. But about two years later, on a cold November night before the snow had come, Alice's car skidded on a stretch of ice that had formed unnoticed beneath a bridge on a two-way stretch of highway, and she ran head on, full speed, into a car coming from the other direction.

Alice survived. After tilting toward death for a year, she gave signs of living again, and she did. But she was never the same. She was all but paralyzed from the hips downward. Her memory was spotty and selective, and she uttered sounds that James had to learn to translate the way a person learns a new language. As months slithered into years, the past crept back with fits and starts into Alice's memory, which, in some ways, made life harder for her, because then she became that much more conscious of her other handicaps. She bore them like a smiling angel most of the time, but unpredictably, out of the blue, she sometimes, for weeks on end, was smothered by depression.

James quit his traveling job right after the accident, got some work near home, and made a nearly full-time vocation of taking care of Alice, once so wonderful. Nobody ever heard a discouraging word from his corner, and the man I had once tabbed a spiritual lightweight showed he was a world-class keeper of commitment.

Alice died fifteen years or so after that one terrible November night, and somebody asked James how he had done it all so patiently when he had gotten such a poor smidgen of everything he had hoped Alice would give to him. He said he had never thought to ask, though he had sometimes asked God why Alice was stuck with living and got nothing back from it.

But, pressed a little, he said it: "I just loved her."

What wondrous love is this that stays when deepest desires go begging?

Then there are Emily and Jason. They had kept a passion stoked, but in bounds, for ten years when, out of nowhere, a virus nobody talks about invaded Jason's loins and knocked his sexual faculties out of connubial commission, rendered him unqualified for the higher registers of sexual love. A microscopic killer, deadly to sex, and no wonder drug to kill it. But Emily has lived with Jason now for fifteen years of noncoital marriage, and if you were to ask her how she manages, I know that she would tell you no more and no less than this: "I love him."

What wondrous love is this that stays after the desires of love are denied?

A lot of our loving *is* a magnificent desire. Someone ignites desires in us and then holds out a promise that he or she can satisfy them. They are desires as deep and strong as we have ever felt. Or can feel. Desires for intimate communion, for being one with another person, totally one, spiritually, sexually one, so that the other can fill us and make us complete.

When a person becomes our hope for what we most wondrously desire, we are in love. And the love we are in is desiring love. It is one of God's better inventions. No one should go through life without it.

Desiring love is a fragile flame, burning bright for a springtime, maybe through summer. But then there is a love we call committed love. It is the love that stays alive through the longest winter.

Human love moves us in two directions, like two currents in a single river, each flowing on its own course.

One love is the current of desire; the other love is the current of commitment.

The current of desiring love is drawn *toward* a promise; it is drawn toward the person who promises to fulfill our deep desires. Nathaniel Branden, in his book *What Love Asks of Us*, defines love as self-centered desire: "Love is the highest, the most intense expression of the . . . 'for me,' 'good for me,' 'beneficial to my life' " human disposition.

The current of commitment moves *from* a promise; it is kept going by a promise to keep on loving when our loving is not satisfying our desires. Marie-Léon Ramlot, in the French *Vocabulary of Biblical Theology* (*Vocabulaire de Theologique Biblique*), fixes on the less selfish way of promised love: "Promise is one of the key words of the language of love. To promise is to pledge one's power and one's faithfulness . . . the commitment of the heart and the generosity of faith."

Two currents. Two directions. Yet both are the currents of love.

Consider for a moment the moods of the first current, desiring love.

> Love delights in her when she is near.
> Love longs for her when she is gone.
> Love hungers for the touch of her flesh.
> Love thirsts for embrace in her spirit.
> Love lives by hope that she will be
> All she promises to me.
> Love dies when she will not be for me
> What I hoped that she would be.

The love of desire! What a gift it is.

Too bad it doesn't last. But it doesn't, not for most people, not after the blessed heat of its early summer days. If someone should promise to desire you forever, don't stake your pension on it. Love born of desire is seldom forever.

The intimate companionship of committed love is what can last a lifetime.

But how do we love another person with a committed love? Is it just raw moral fiber that holds us in a relationship no matter how badly it disappoints us? Sticking with what we are stuck with until a merciful death parts us: is this commitment love?

Yes, in a way, it can be something like a will to survive,

sometimes, when life gets terribly tough, and one part of us wants to pack up and leave the scene.

Committed love is a will to give love a chance at permanent tenure. But gutsy sticking is not what committed love is *all* about.

Commitments build the strong walls that hold up a partnership. But these strong outer walls are important only because an inner life of caring love can be nurtured inside them. The walls give care a structure for survival. Sticking it out provides a place for love to come home to after it has wandered a while. And maybe lost its way. But making it last is only a way of giving people a chance to make it good.

What, then, is there to committed love besides sticking to a relationship? What else does commitment do to keep love alive and well—or to heal it when it gets sick—or maybe to resurrect it when it has died?

Committed love is a paradoxical power. Paradoxical? Yes, paradoxical, because it is a power to surrender. A *power* to surrender? Yes, power, because sometimes it takes a lot of strength to surrender.

But everything depends on what you surrender.

Committed love is a power to surrender our right to get what we desire so that the person we love can get what he or she needs.

Let's slow down here and take the last sentence in bits. We surrender our *right*. Our right to what we desire. For the sake of the *need* the *other person* has. When my desire conflicts with your need, I will opt for your needs—if my love is committed love.

We are talking about a love that reaches out beyond our own wants into the other person's needs. Keeps reaching. Keeps trying to understand what the other's real needs are, keeps looking for them, asking about them, patiently prying behind the pride that hides them, listening for the coded messages, waiting for the right time for plain words, staying there with her, because I know that she, like me, has deep, deep needs that leave her poor of spirit if they are not met.

Committed love is for the winter of life's unfairness, when we feel drained of a dream that didn't come true, for the wormwood season of our desire's disillusion.

Careful now, we must not misunderstand the terms of surrender. Committed love is *not* the surrender of our needs for the sake of the other person's desires. Committed love does not turn us into stooges for another person's whims—obedient servants of his or her brutality—suckers for his or her betrayals. Nor is it a set-up for putdowns.

But sometimes when I surrender my right to have what I desire, I can *feel* as if I am surrendering one of my truest needs. I need help to see the real difference.

Do you really *need* a voluptuous sex life or do you only *want* it badly? Do you really *need* somebody fascinating to talk to you every night or do you only *want* it badly? Do you really *need* a partner who makes you feel like a terrific human being or do you only *want* one?

Well, if not the *Alleluia Chorus* at every bedding down, at least *Eine Kleine Nachtmusik* for you now and then. And if not somebody who makes scintillating conversation every night before the burning hearth, how about one who smiles your way over a TV dinner? And if not a partner who lifts your self-esteem a couple of notches at every breakfast, at least one who doesn't clobber your self-image in front of company. Not asking too much.

Desiring love does not always reach for the sky. It can make accommodations. Most of us settle for a decent earthly compromise, so long as our cup is at least half-full.

The question is, how can committed love keep flowing when the current of desiring love stops running our way?

The answer is, by blending desire with care.

Care comes quietly alive when the winds of desire hush, and I hear the whisper of need.

But care has lyrics of its own.

Care is love's investment in another person's needs.
Care is love's permission for the other to walk to the beat of a different drummer.
Care is love's gratitude for the other's unexpected gifts.
Care is love's flexibility to go where another needs to go.
Care is love's firmness to stay close by when the other cannot move.
Care is love's generosity to give when the other speaks of needs.
Care is love's presence when being there matters most.
Care is love's power to survive the death of desire.

The miracle of care is that when I have gotten over my unfulfilled desires, I discover that taking care is gratifying, in a very

different way, but just as gratifying in its way as expected pleasure is. Not as exciting, not as erotic, not as crazy making either,
but in its own way more fulfilling over the long haul.

Her needs *become* my desires. This is what loving care, caring
love, is about.

Caring love is more than doing things for someone. Care is
also a respect that holds back and lets another be. Caring love
respects her right to be her very real self, unshadowed by me,
in the light of the sun that shines equally bright on us both. It
knows that she has a valid claim to be left alone to be who and
what she is. It respects her inalienable right to be treated with
honor and reverence even when desiring love for her is dead or
dying.

It is care that also keeps bright the memory of yesterday's
desires. Memory is the mysterious power to resurrect in October
a desire that died in April. A memory is a living thing; it blends
what was with what is now. And when the winds of desire are
not strong enough to "twirl one red leaf," memory sweetens
what is with the scent of what used to be. And committed love
says, "Thanks for the memory."

Let me tell you of the two loves of Eric Zorg—of his desiring
love and his committed love. It will make everything clear.

Eric loved his wife, Karen, for fifteen years in an idyll of
yeasty desire.

Let it be said in honesty that jealousy sometimes played bad
tricks on them in the darker nooks of their eros. Still, it is true
that Eric felt the flow of his desire moving like a white water
rapid toward Karen alone, toward all she embodied in the flex-
uous tautness of her flesh and all she ensouled in the breezy
freedom of her spirit.

They loved each other well.

But five years ago Karen's sprightly sexuality was slackened
a step by a nettlesome lapse in memory, mostly a forgetting of
names, then of dates, and then slowly of things so near and
precious to her that, in her bright interludes, she knew something was happening to her that she wanted, above all, not to
happen.

Early on, before Alzheimer's disease occupied the heartland
of her life, she still was able to offer an occasional seductive
promise to Eric. And she still did her first mate's chores on their

thirty-five-footer, her fumbling with the gear only making her salty grit the more precious in his eyes, while they skimmed the lazy Pacific swells from Catalina Island back to Marina Del Rey. But that was more than four years ago, when weekends on the ocean felt like an hour spent too soon.

Now every hour is a shadowed day.

Karen's once vital body and luminous spirit no longer signal to Eric that he is of all men most favored. She does not talk anymore; Eric calls her Karen, but the name is a scratch of sound to her now, and she makes no answer to it.

Eric maneuvers small spoonfuls of bland mush into her mouth several times each day, playing gentle tricks on her mouth to get the spoon inside, only to have her spit half of it, half-munched, on her baby bib. He cleans her diapers and wakes often during the night to cover her shoulders with the blanket she has tossed off in her fidgety sleep. Does she dream? Does she know Eric is there? That he who is there is Eric? He cannot tell.

He has moved his office into his house, and works out of it there now, nagging and nursing his insurance accounts while keeping one eye on Karen, in case she is seized by one of her sudden, strange urges to wander, sometimes far, where no one knows her, outside the house. His friends tell him he should put Karen in an institution.

What is there in the fabric of this man, this ordinary man who still has the same deep desires all ordinary men have, what is there that binds him to the side of this mockery of the woman who promised once that she would satisfy his desires forever?

He has as much right to happiness as any other man. Why does he not shuffle her off to professional custodians, and seek a new love to meet his unslaked desires? What compels him to stay with Karen in the dawnless darkness of her soul's lingering night?

Committed love, and only that, is what keeps Eric at her side. He *cares* for Karen.

She calls out a need she cannot speak and he answers back with a care he cannot explain. Care, love's survivor of desires that died with a shining yesterday, is the miracle behind Eric's caring presence in his darker today.

Desire is spent. There is nothing of her he desires. How could he desire this stranger, this mewling infant who spits up on her pillow? It is care for a restless body whose irrational spirit seems sometimes to mock him like a demon chortling over a lost soul.

It is care that keeps *respect* for her.

He respects the God-like being hidden somewhere inside this frail mindless form of a woman to whom he once said those most daring words: I will be there with you. He cannot see her real self, feel her magic, or hear her music anymore. He just believes that she is there, ravaged but not destroyed by the Alzheimer syndrome.

And it is with care that he *remembers* her.

What he remembers is alive as the love that fulfilled his past. Who she was dances with what she is now. His life with the real Karen is not dead. It is alive in the flitting images on the screen of his remembrance. His memory gives him a savory after-taste of what he once desired and she once gave him.

There are cynics who say that Eric only does what he does because he knows he will be more miserable still if he does anything else; he is only choosing the lesser of two miseries. Nothing heroic about that. Maybe so. And it is true that he sometimes rages in his soul's dark room, stifling complaints to a silent God too long gone on leave of absence, muffling a wish he dares not utter, a prayer for Karen to die.

Committed love is seldom pure; we will not have it without a tangle of conflicting cries, without muttering our muffled complaints. It is always alloyed with the coarser stuff of unsatisfied desires. But even compromised, it is the secret power for sticking with what we are stuck with when the fun has gone out of it and we know that sorrow may stay to the end.

What I've said in this chapter is simple, elemental, and a foundation for everything else that is still to be said. Commitment is a way of loving as the fire of desire slowly burns down, and we feel a little cheated because the best thing we have ever wanted is passing away. But caring is commitment's way of loving, not getting what someone promises us, but giving what someone needs. And when respect and good memories are added to care, we have the makings of enduring love. The makings of a love that lasts, and more, a love that makes life enduringly beautiful.

Part 2

THE COMMITTED RELATIONSHIPS

CHAPTER 5

Creating Our Own Identity

What life is about for most of us is a search for ourselves. We want to know who we are. And how to define ourselves to others. So we spend our lives finding out.

We are looking for a personal hub that holds us together as the wheels of our lives keep turning.

We change, we accept change, we want change. No healthy person wants to be stuck forever with what he or she was in the past. Or is now. If we don't change we get stale, complacent, and mired in our sins and miseries. But if we don't hold ourselves together while we change, we lose our balance.

Let me speak for myself. I want my life to be more like a continuous line _____ than a series of unconnected dots. . . . . A curved line, yes, a line that twists and turns around a thousand corners, but still, somehow, stays connected all the while.

I want links and contacts between my yesterdays and my tomorrows. Growth, yes, change, of course, but what a zany life it would be if I couldn't recognize my real self in the images of my past.

It is a miracle, sort of, that the boy I see on a wrinkled snapshot, that scrawny matchstick with pants on, skinny as a baby sparrow, is actually the same person as the silver old bird writing this sentence. How remarkable, and yet how important to me, that I and that clothespole are one and the same person.

But the changes we pass through are not the only reason we keep searching for the abiding self we are.

We are so confoundingly complicated. And confused.

One of me is a wily rake; the other is a simple saint. One of me is laughingly healthy; the other is a pouting neurotic. One of me is a romantic poet, sighing for the perfect love; the other is a practical realist, content to love faithfully, if imperfectly. One of me is vulgar enough to shock my best friends; the other is refined enough to get along in all the proper places. One of me is a true believer; the other is a wondering doubter. I carry such contradictions within myself that I must confuse the angels.

But where is the *real* me? I would know my real self better if I could just be more consistent, more simple, put together so all the parts nicely fit.

Where can we find our enduring selves beneath all our metamorphoses and conflicts?

I have come to the conclusion that we find our real self in the continuing stories we are writing with our lives.

We are all writing our stories; and each of us has to write his or her own. I cannot write my parents' stories, any more than they could have written mine. I cannot write my children's stories, though there have been times that I have wanted to. I can write only mine.

The trick is to write a continuing story. A story with a plot that has a central character. Not a collection of unconnected episodes about a collection of unconnected characters.

Writing a continuing story out of my life depends on whether I dare to make commitments to people and care enough to keep the commitments I make. And whether I accept other people's commitments to me as gifts that contribute to my story.

In fact, who we are always begins with somebody's commitment to us.

Who am I? I am Rena Smedes's boy. I have an identity because a woman committed herself to me when I was "mewling and puking" in her arms, a sickly, bawling, undernourished, skin-and-bones baby. I am somebody because a woman was there for me, touching me, feeding me, warming me, hushing me, and letting me believe that she would be there for me again, and again, when I needed her. And I have a self because the same woman kept her commitment to me.

It is not as though I always accepted her commitment to me as the raw material for the beginning of my story. I often demanded—as a condition for accepting her—that she be a different person than the real, complicated human being she was.

I did not want her to be a woman who could not provide me with a father. I did not want her to be gone away from home, working so hard and getting so tired that she had to dig terribly deep to mine enough energy for me when she was at hand. I did not want her to talk with a Frisian accent, like a foreigner. And I did not want her to think so poorly of herself that she could not find it in her to permit me to think well of myself. I wanted her to fit my fantasies of what a mother should be like.

But I grew up and put away my childish yen to recreate my one and only mother into something she never had been or could have been. I accepted her as the one who made a commitment of care to me and kept it even when keeping it was a titanic challenge for her. I accepted her as God's way of beginning my story with her commitment.

So the first scene in the story of my life defines me forever: I am the skinny kid to whom the widow Rena Smedes committed herself.

But I am also writing my story out of my own commitments to other people.

Whenever I make an important commitment to a person, I begin a new chapter in my story. I will not know the full meaning of my commitment until I have finished my tale. Margaret Farley makes the same point in her book *Personal Commitments*. "The ultimate meaning . . . of the promise I make today can be clear only at the end of my life; and the meaning of my life at its end will be different because I made this promise today." When I make my commitment, I put myself in a stream that flows in a certain direction. I won't know for sure until I get to the end what it really meant when I entered the stream.

What finally comes of our commitments really depends on a thousand small choices we make in the *process* of keeping them.

Three years ago I made a commitment to my publisher that I would write a book about commitment. I didn't have an inkling at the time what my commitment would come to mean. What gives meaning to my commitment is what I decide to write day by day, sentence by sentence, word by word.

I make countless choices about this book every day I work at it. I write certain sentences. I keep some, but I throw others away; they won't be part of the book. I grab hold of an idea; but it doesn't connect with what I wrote earlier, and I let it go again. Then, suddenly, another thought seizes me, a sheer gift, and it seems to fit, so I write it down.

One day the book will be finished; I will have kept my commitment. Then I will know what it meant when I made my original commitment to write it. But I am deciding what it will mean each time I write another word.

It's something like this with the stories we write with our lives. We make commitments to people. Each commitment leads us into a particular relationship. But we determine what each commitment will contribute to our stories by the choices we make midstream, *after* we have made our commitment.

We want to chuck some episodes; we don't want them in our stories. That is, we don't want them to tell us who we are. So we forgive ourselves, and start over again. We edit out a part of our stories. And start again at the point just before we made a false move. Forgiveness gives us the right to edit out the bad episodes from our stories.

The main thing is that the episodes we do keep all fit together as our own continuing stories.

So I will ask once more: who am I? And I will tell you.

I am the person who committed himself to a woman named Doris more than thirty years ago; I am Doris's husband, that's who I really am.

I am sure I did not know what it really meant for me to make that commitment at the time I made it. I unconsciously assumed that everything—the world, Doris, my feelings—would stay pretty much the same as they were then. But nothing has stayed the same. Our world has changed, beyond belief. Our places in the world have changed. Our bodies have changed. Our thoughts and our feelings have changed. So much has changed, and all in ways neither of us could have predicted when we first committed ourselves.

If you want to know the real me, you would have to know about a thousand small decisions I have made along the way, some good ones, some bad ones, some creative ones, some destructive ones, that have sewn a pattern into the fabric that I chose when I committed myself to her.

But the making and keeping of that one commitment is one of the most important plot lines in my continuing story.

Who am I?

I am the person who, with Doris, committed himself to adopt three children. We didn't know what it was going to mean when we did this, any more than Columbus knew what he was getting himself into when he set off to find the East Indies. But our commitment set us in a stream to swim with *these* particular children, not with three ideal kids we might have fantasized. And we thrashed and bungled our way through the years of tears and laughter, unceasing caring, unceasing loving, pointless worrying, keeping the commitment we made to these three human beings. We weren't the parents we might have been, we were only the parents we were able to be, certainly the only parents they had.

It will be a while before we or they know all that our original commitment means for our life stories. But I know that I am writing my story out of the raw material of that single commitment Doris and I made when we took those kids into our lives.

Who am I?

I am the person who committed himself to close friends. And I am the person who committed himself to his students. And I am the person who committed himself to God upon discovering that he had already committed himself to me.

Never mind that my commitments are sometimes half-baked, never mind that I keep them sometimes against tired impulses to pack it all in. The point is that I locate myself, identify myself, and keep in touch with my real self, in the significant commitments I have made and keep on making to significant people in my life.

You see only the outline of my real self, of course. I haven't painted color into the flesh. Or penciled in the wrinkles. You cannot tell from my commitments whether I would be any fun at your party, or whether you would like to play golf with me, or whether you would enjoy a long talk with me. And you cannot tell how I feel.

There are a lot of things I could tell you about the feelings I have felt while trying to keep my commitments. I could tell about sadness that swallowed me whole when what I wanted most was taken from me, about a stewing anger I foolishly nurtured too long about things I could not change, about fears that kept me awake at night, and about depressions that wasted my joy during the day. Feelings that drove me to act in ways that might have driven a less committed wife to pack her bags and leave me.

All of these feelings give spice and vinegar to who I am. And I know that I cannot know myself if I deny my own feelings or if I stifle them.

It took me a long time to accept my feelings as part of who I really was. I let the bad feelings, the nagging, gnawing, guilty feelings, tell me who I really was. But I was afraid to truly own the good feelings, the loving, warm, vulnerable feelings, though they danced just behind the curtain of my consciousness, longing to come on stage to tell me in the liquid music of the spirit that they belonged to me.

So I needed to be reconciled with my best feelings. And I was.

But are my feelings the whole me, the me of my continuing story?

I feel so many things. I feel good, I feel bad. I feel happy, I feel sad. I feel bored, I feel excited. I feel flat, I feel alive. I feel free, I feel trapped. I feel innocent, I feel guilty. And if I told you all I felt, we would have a very, very long conversation.

So many mixed-up feelings, flowing in and out of my being, I can't tell them apart. They are too fuzzy, too slippery, too changeable to give me a clear view of myself. And if all you knew about me was my feelings, you would know only a small part of me, the way you know a small part of a great novel if you read only the love scenes.

Nor do other people's feelings about me tell me who I am. Erik Erikson—the psychologist who has taught us so much about the search for our own identity—warns us against trying to find ourself by looking at our image in the pool of other people's feelings.

I could kill myself trying to get people to feel good about me, so that I can feel good about myself. I would be forever wearing masks in front of people, seducing them to have nice feelings about me. And I would be back on the circuit day after day in my silly search for myself in other people's looking glasses. But I would never find my*self* there.

It is not what other people *feel about me* that ties my story together. I write my story out of what I *am* for other people.

Nor can I write my story by running away from the roles I play.

I saw a movie a few years ago called *My Dinner with André*, hailed by some critics as a movie with a message for our times. The entire film is a dinner conversation between two New York playwrights who play themselves.

The narrator works at his craft and lives in an East Side apartment, trying to pay his rent, read some books, keep a relationship alive at home, and be somebody in the theater. André is an old friend, almost forgotten, who shows up out of nowhere and invites him for dinner downtown; they go, and we listen to them talk as André tells his old friend about his treks through the Mideast, in search of his uncommitted self.

"Things can go dead on you," he says, "and when it happens you have to become a kind of hobo or something, go out on the road like Kerouac. . . . I said to myself, 'I've been acting the role of a husband.' So I stopped performing.

"Imagine what life could be like for you. If you feel like walking out on the person you live with, you walk out. And if you feel like coming back, you come back.

"People hold on to these images of themselves as fathers or husbands as if these roles could give them some firm ground. But what does that mean . . . to be a wife, or a husband, or a son. They all go away. Where are they? Where is that son?"

So speaks André, he of the unfettered life, fluid, flowing, free.

The dinner is over. The narrator is envious of André. He leaves. And he takes a leap toward his own freedom by blowing more money than he can afford on a cab, instead of taking the subway, going home the way he feels like going, but home, nonetheless, back to his work, back to his roles. On his way home he passes the store that his father once owned, the places he belonged to when he was a kid, sees the threads in his own story, and begins to doubt André's gospel of the uncommitted life.

I met André just lately. He told me that he had found inner freedom to be, just to *be*. Be what? Be nothing. Just *be*, couldn't I see? But I couldn't really find this *be-ing* anywhere. He was feeling without substance, a character without a story.

There is another way of thinking about the roles we play.

They are parts we create in our *real* life stories, not parts we act out in a performance on the stage. Shakespeare says, "All the world's a stage, and all the men and women merely players." But that is metaphor. Reality is something else. My roles are the callings I hear, the needs I meet, the care I give, the love I offer. I am the *real* me when I play these parts.

The fact of the matter is that I discover my real self when I keep creating my role as imperfect husband and father in an imperfect family. I discovered my real self when I sat up night after night with a four-year-old asthmatic boy as he fought off death in his terrible struggle for breath. I discovered myself in the terrors of loving a hothead adolescent who was dying of a wish to love me and love herself. I discovered myself in these roles that I created out of my commitments to people.

Running from committed roles into the tents of tentativity turns our life stories into an endless setting up and breaking up of camp, fits and starts, one thing after another with no links between them, and a loss of self in the aimless turning.

What makes it possible for a real person to write a continuing story out of his or her life is "the capacity to commit himself to concrete affiliations . . . to abide by such commitments, even though they call for significant sacrifice and compromises." This is Erik Erikson, in *Childhood and Society*. And my sense of reality echoes, "Yes, it is true."

Here is a corker of a sentence from philosopher Hannah Arendt's book *The Human Condition*. It was my springboard into the thoughts I have written in this chapter: "Without being bound to the fulfillment of our promises, we would never be able to keep our identities; we would be condemned to wander helplessly and without direction in the darkness of each person's lonely heart, caught in its contradictions and equivocalities."

Caught in the contradictions of my lonely heart! Of course there *are* contradictions in my life. But to be caught in them, so that there is nothing to me besides the contradictions, nowhere a clear sign of a consistent self abiding through my wanderings? Jean-Paul Sartre pictured hell as eternal confinement in a room without an exit. But hell could be a life with nothing but exits, aimless wandering, never knowing who we are because we are unconnected to who we've been in the stories we write.

A woman creates a family and then cannot find it in herself

to stay with it; she leaves an important segment of herself behind and need not hope to find herself again unless she makes and keeps new commitments to other significant relationships. A man passes through one job after another, important jobs too, a corporate executive moving from one corporation to another, improving his fringe benefits each time he moves, but he never commits himself to anyone, and never finds himself in his fringe benefits. He will have produced, at the end, a disconnected series of suburban sitcoms to remember, not a continuing story of a committed life. Unless he is converted to commitment while he still has a chance to write some new chapters. A child runs away from home to find his own unique identity and ends up losing touch with his own self until he somehow comes to terms with himself as the child of the family he has fled.

I remember a line from *A Man for All Seasons*, Thomas Bolt's brilliant play about Thomas More. In one scene More is explaining to his daughter Margaret why he cannot go back on an oath he took: "When a man makes a promise, Meg, he puts himself into his own hands, like water. And if he opens his fingers to let it out, he need not hope to find himself again." Yes, Thomas More, you were right; in our hearts we know you were.

We do not quickly find the definition of our true selves. But the end of all our searching will be here, where we began, at this familiar place: we will create ourselves in the commitments we dare to make and care enough to keep.

CHAPTER 6

Making Friendships That Last

We all want someone who knows us better than anyone else does, and yet accepts us, enjoys us, needs us, holds nothing back from us, keeps our secrets, and is there for us when we want to be near her.

We all seem to need at least one close friend. Even people who believe they ought to love everybody need special people they want to be close to just because they like them. And are liked by them. It's different from charity; we ought to feel charity for needy people. But we want somebody as a close friend because we like her, not because she needs our kindness.

I'm talking about a close friend, a best friend, not a casual friend or a friendly acquaintance. It's hard to describe the precise difference between a close friend and a casual friend. But this doesn't matter much because if you have a close friend, you will know the difference.

It's a matter of preference. A close friend is somebody who prefers to have us around, is partial to us, makes us his favorite. We talk about things together we don't talk about with other people. We do things together that we don't want to do with anyone else, at least not as much as we want to do them with each other. Friends stick with their favorites; that's the way of friendship; it always discriminates.

There is a friend that sticks to us closer than a brother, the Bible says, telling us as much about brothers as it does about friends. Not a surprising revelation, in fact, because *most* friends do stick closer to us than brothers do, or sisters.

But is there a friend who lasts as long as a brother does? Maybe until death? Are we expecting too much when we want close friends to be our friends forever in a world where almost everything is only for the time being?

WE WANT FRIENDSHIP TO LAST

I had a best friend early on, the first friend I ever had, and he stuck a lot closer to me than my brother did. His name was Clary Kramer; he and I were as close as any two boys could be, I think. We shared everything, did everything together, except go to church, and that didn't matter much to us.

The Depression had become a way of life in our neighborhood when we were growing up. Clary's dad had a part-time job fetching and delivering clothes for Eastbrook Dry Cleaners. My dad was dead. Both of our families were poor, though we didn't think being poor was anything out of the ordinary.

We lived across some vacant lots from each other; he could see my house from his front porch, and I could see his house from our back stoop, and we walked a path bare through the weeds between them.

We played hockey with crumpled tin cans for pucks and worn-out brooms for hockey sticks; Amity Street, my street, was paved with concrete, so we used it for our rink. We made scooters out of broken roller skates nailed to a board. And we made skiis out of barrel staves we found in the trash behind a butcher shop. So we spent a lot of our time looking around in trash for the stuff we played with.

We were the Katzenjammer Kids, if not the Damon and Pythias, of our neighborhood.

One game we often played when we ran out of ideas on a muggy summer day was mumblety-peg, a game that people have played for centuries, in a hundred variations, but always with a simple double-bladed jackknife. (Not your Boy Scout knife with its clutter of can openers, and screw drivers, and such things.)

In our version the players squatted on the lawn, facing each other. We shoved the smaller blade—that blade sticking out at a right angle from the handle while the larger blade poked straight ahead—in the sod, put our index finger under the far end of the handle, and flipped the knife, end over end, into the air.

What you wanted was for the knife to land with the blade sticking in the turf, handle up.

(In the original version the winner got to drive a peg into the ground with the knife, and the loser had to pull the peg out with his teeth while the winner paddled his backside. And so the game was called mumble-the-peg or, where we lived, mumblety-peg.)

We played make-believe baseball. If the knife landed with the bigger blade piercing the turf, handle standing straight up, and the smaller blade horizontal, clear of the ground, you had yourself a homerun; a knife lying flat on the grass was, naturally, an out; and so on.

When the grass was tall and thick, it could hold the handle pointed upward, so it was hard to tell sometimes whether the blade was stuck in the ground deep enough to hold up the knife or whether it was held up, somewhat slanted, but still not flat, by the grass.

One afternoon I flipped the knife and made what I figured was a homerun. Clary claimed that the blade was not stuck deep enough into the ground, that in fact the handle was being held at an angle by the tall grass, and that I was out.

A tough judgment call! With no umpire to call it. So we did what any two boys might do to settle any unsettleable argument. We had a fight.

I was getting the better of him, had him down, belly up, with me sitting on his belly, crouching, with both knees on the ground beside him. But his arms were free, he had a good swing, horizontally, and he was holding the knife in his right hand, big blade out.

He made a full, rounded, side-armed swipe and got me on the knee, a clean stab, not a slice, but a puncture, in the side of the knee bone.

I got up off his stomach and hobbled home, dragging my aching right leg. He got up off his back and slouched across the field that separated his house from mine. He did not talk to me. I did not talk to him. Not a word, neither of us could get any sound out, no yelling, no bawling, two friends hushed into a hunch that they were breaking up.

I think both of us sensed, on the spot, in a single blink, that we were not going to be friends anymore.

We did not become friends again, ever. All the way through school we walked different paths with different friends; he had his crowd, I had mine, and we never crossed over. Now and then we would bump into each other when we couldn't help it, but we were always glad to get away, like one-time lovers who run into each other on a busy street and know without saying so that there is no point in trying to bring back a lost love.

But I have never gotten over it. Whenever I am in my hometown, to this day, I ask about Clary. What has happened to him? Where did he end up? And whom did he end up with? What's he doing now?

Why do I keep asking about him? Why—after all these long years—haven't I forgotten about that trifling fight over a judgment call at mumblety-peg? Why has it stuck, as a melancholy stitch, on the border of my life's fabric? A little stitch, sure, but still a sad one.

I think it is because I want friendship to last. And I feel cheated when it doesn't. If life were right, it seems to me, good friendships would last.

We want a friend who sticks with us when we get down and being around us is not fun. Who will not stop liking us when we feel unlikable. We all have secret worries about our powers to keep a friend. James Kavanaugh's poem catches all our doubts:

Will you be my friend?
There are so many reasons why you never should:
Often I'm too serious, seldom predictably the same,
Sometimes cold and distant, probably I'll always change.
I bluster and brag, seek attention like a child,
I brood and pout, my anger can be wild. . . .
I shake a little most every day
Because I'm more frightened than the strangers ever know,
And if at times I show my trembling side,
I wonder, will you be my friend?

And we worry after we have moved away from each other and we do not play tennis together anymore, or share our hopes for our kids, or bitch about the unfairness of fortune. Will our friendship last? And as we wonder, we know we want it to last. We want a friend who sticks, not only as close, but as long as a brother.

For when we lose a close friend, we feel like a dancer whose partner suddenly leaves her, and she has to go on dancing alone. Kierkegaard says that to lose a friend makes us feel like a hyphenated word when the second part is erased and only an embarrassing half-   is left. We hang there, like the hyphen, waiting for the other half to come back.

But you can't count on her—or him—to come back, not the way things go in our world, where every good thing that comes has to leave us one day.

WE DON'T REALLY EXPECT FRIENDSHIPS TO LAST FOREVER

Even the way we become friends is a hint that we do not believe that they are meant to last forever.

For instance, we don't usually arrange a ceremony to begin a friendship with solemn vows. Fancy asking the rector at St. Mark's to arrange a "friendship ceremony" for you at the cathedral. Tell the rector you want a high church service, a cleric well robed, a grand organ, with the slow strains coaxing both of you, arm in arm, as befits friends, toward the altar, before which the two of you will vow a solemn covenant of friendship "until death doth us part." A traditional rector will probably think you are a bit crazy, but will tell you in sympathetic rectorial tones, "I surely do respect your feelings. But that sort of thing is not done in this church."

It happened once in a while, in the olden days, that friends vowed to be friends forever, no matter what. Maybe you remember the biblical story of Jonathan and David, and how they took an oath to friendship forever. "Jonathan made a covenant with David because he loved him . . . ." And they both banked on that sweet swearing when the times turned treacherous and friendship was tested in blood. A great story, and worth thinking about; maybe it *would* help friends to stay together always if they swore an oath at the beginning.

But it isn't the way most of us get to be friends. We are more likely to stray into friendship, fumble into it almost by accident. We meet, needy, ready for a friend, and we feel each other's pulse, delicately, discreetly, as the openings come. We look each other over, discover that we talk the same language, that we agree on what is important in life, that we like to do the same sorts of things, and that we get special satisfaction from doing them with each other. And so we fumble into friendship just by hitting it off.

It is the same when casual friends become best friends; we do not step beyond the casual stage into best friendships the way people move from being lovers to becoming wife and husband. We get to be best friends, as Lillian Rubin notes in her book *Just Friends*, by a kind of grafting and a growing together as we learn to trust each other, feel safe with each other, understand each other, admire each other, maybe even envy each other, and simply expect each other to be there to do things we especially like to do together.

If a times comes when we don't feel safe in it anymore, can't count on each other, get too involved with other relationships, maybe fall in love and get married, we gradually remove the life support systems and let the friendship die, let it die with dignity if we are lucky, but die anyhow.

And when it dies neither of us feels that we have violated a sacred commitment. Preachers do not tell us that the country is going to the dogs because of the decline of friendship. Friendships die and nobody clucks a moral cluck. Nor do we formalize the ending of friendships. Popes do not annul friendships, the courts do not issue a decree of divorce between friends.

All of this suggests that we do not really expect friendships to last permanently.

And, after all, maybe friendship is not really the sort of relationship that is *meant* to last?

ARE FRIENDSHIPS EVER FOREVER?

What goes into the making of any friendship? What are the ingredients that mesh ordinary people into this wonderful, this tender, this too fragile relationship? And why can't we count on it to last?

There are three kinds of friendship, as Aristotle saw it. One of them is a friendship based on affection: friends like each other and enjoy each other. Another is a friendship based on usefulness: friends do things for each other. And a third kind is based on character: friends admire each other.

I think every real friendship is a mixture of all three ingredients. It's just that the blend changes from one friendship to another. But there is a lot to say for Aristotle's list, enough anyway to see why none of his three kinds of friendship can last long if it doesn't have commitment as the bonding agent. Let's look at each of them.

FRIENDSHIPS OF AFFECTION: WE LIKE EACH OTHER

Someone gets special pleasure out of being in your company. Your presence adds to her enjoyment of whatever she is doing with you, you are a joy to her. And you make her feel better. You are a comfort to her. This is affection, and it makes for close friends.

Maybe it is just the sort of person you are, your personality, your style; it blends well with the sort of person she is. She feels comfortable with you, the way a person gets comfortable with an old shoe; the longer you are around, the better you fit. You make a friend feel good in almost any situation.

She may rate other people higher on the character scale, and you may not be the smartest person she knows; no matter, she likes being with you, even if she isn't sure why.

It isn't as if she looks in your eyes and tells you that she really likes being with you. In fact, she doesn't think about you much when she is with you, just as she doesn't think about the comfortable shoes she's wearing. You and she are concentrating on your tennis shots. Or on getting a party organized. Maybe you are arguing about why God allows so much pain in the world, or you are just rooting for your kids at a soccer game. The point is that you get pleasure out of doing these things *with* each other. And at the end of a long afternoon, you may just say, "That was good, let's do it again."

And we are not close friends just because we like *doing* the same *things*. I have known people who liked fishing as much as I do, but they are the last persons with whom I would want to go fishing. There has to be something about the person himself that makes doing something fun because I am doing it *with him*.

We like *each other*, of course. If I wanted to be with you because I liked you, and you were only willing to be with me because you felt sorry for me, we couldn't be friends. Reciprocity is the key.

Too bad liking each other a lot can't make friendships last for life. Two things get in the way.

For one thing, even best friends move to new jobs in new locations, and get too far apart to play together or work together. So they find new people in their new place, people whom they like and with whom they enjoy doing things. Alvin Toffler warns us, in *Future Shock*, that in the future—which has since become the present—all our friendships would be ad hoc: here, now, and over with when the company sends one of us to another plant, or when we join another church or move to another neighborhood. Friendship for this place, this time, and as long as we stay put. But not much longer.

For another thing, friends change, and they may discover that they have stopped liking the new version of each other. Everybody's friend has something unlikable sneaking about in her personality. We discover it in each other sooner or later, and sometimes it annoys us too much to put up with it. Jane liked a lot of things about her friend Thelma, even though she was forever borrowing her things and hardly ever returned them. But she tired of having to ask her to give them back, and her nagging gradually siphoned the pleasure out of their friendship for both of them. So, as they stopped liking each other, they gradually slipped out of friendship.

Aristotle says in his *Ethics* that friendships of affection fade away "as soon as the reasons for which the friends loved each other no longer present themselves." And such thought led Gilbert Meilander glumly, with a touch of exaggeration, to put it on the line, in his book, *Friendship*: "Fidelity and friendship are incompatible."

In any case, liking each other is not enough to turn two people into life-long friends. Life-long friendships need commitment.

FRIENDSHIPS OF USEFULNESS: WE DO THINGS FOR EACH OTHER

Good friends do favors for each other. Most of my friends do more for me than I do for them. Not more than I want to do for them. But more than I can do for them. So being their friend is an advantage for me. They are not my friends because they do me favors; they want to do me favors because they are my friends.

But some people become friends simply because of what they can do for each other. Business friends, for instance. They give each other tax advice and investment tips. They help each other make contacts at conventions. They exchange notes on where to buy equipment at discount, and they gossip about competitors. What an advantage to have one another as friends!

But that is about as far as it goes. They don't share each other's family problems. Henry Morton, who runs a computer store, is a friend of Gerry Mansfield, a sales representative at IBM; they do a lot for each other. But Henry never tells Gerry that his heart is breaking because his teenage daughter is pregnant. And Sally Nordew, who has her own accounting firm, is a friend of Richard Holbert, a tax attorney; they both benefit from their relationship. But Sally sees Richard only over a lunch once a week or so, and she never tells him that she is worried sick that she might have cancer.

Some people make friends only with people who can be useful to them. Franklin D. Roosevelt loved to have people around him, cronies, politicians, intellectuals, all kinds. But we are told that he made friends only with people who could help him keep his rendezvous with destiny. One historian (Doris Kearns Goodwin, in *The Fitzgeralds and the Kennedys*) says of him: "At bottom, for all his warmth and capacity to make friends instantly, FDR was a man without a deep commitment to anyone. He enjoyed people . . . but he rarely gave himself to them." Maybe the great and powerful people of the world pay for being great and powerful by missing out on committed friendship.

Friendships of usefulness can be flavored with feelings of affection. They can even become intimate. But getting close is not the same as being committed.

Being useful to each other keeps two people together only as long as the advantage is enjoyed by both of them, and doesn't get too one-sided. And the trade-off eventually does get uneven. One of the friends ends up doing a lot more for his friend than his friend does for him. Or her. One of them may get fired, or lose his clout, and not be able to do much for the other. When it happens his friend may stop calling, never have time for lunch, and a chill wind may blow the friendship away.

These friendships do not depend on what people *are* to each other, but on what they *do for* each other. They are based on a kind of service contract; the friend who is giving more service than he is getting is free to cancel the contract with honor. So this is one reason why friendships based on reciprocated services don't usually last for life. They lack personal commitment.

FRIENDSHIPS OF CHARACTER: WE ADMIRE EACH OTHER

I admire most of my friends. I even envy them; I wish I had some of their good qualities. In fact, I don't think I would want to be friends with people who did not have something about them that I admired.

But admiration needs to be shared. I like people whom I admire to admire me as well. Admire at least something about me. Otherwise it's hard for me to be their friend.

I have a good friend whom everyone admires. One reason that everyone admires him is that he has a radar in his mind that picks up something worthy beneath the skin of almost everyone he knows, and he finds loving ways to tell them what sorts of nice things he sees in them. But what makes me his friend and not his fan is that he sees good stuff in me too, and now and then he lets me know what he sees.

If I admired a person who saw nothing in me worth admiring, I could be his fan. Maybe even his disciple. But not his friend. To be friends we need to admire each other.

Aristotle thought that friends who admire each other's character are likely to have a lasting friendship. Why? Because character doesn't change very much. Good people do not usually become bad people. So if we are friends because we admire each other's character, we could be friends for life.

But not even mutual admiration is, by itself, enough to keep a friendship alive that long. For one thing, we discover somewhere along the line that even people we admire have feet of clay. The best of us is flawed. Our flaws show through eventually; we disappoint our friends, and sometimes their disappointment hurts enough to wound our friendship. Or even worse, we may discover that the traits we so much admired were put-ons, cosmetics hiding a shabby interior. And we cannot count on any friendship to survive the feeling of being conned.

Besides, even friends who admire each other a lot drift apart when one of them moves to another part of the country. If I move away, don't see my friend again for five years, and do not stay in close touch, our friendship is likely to die of malnutrition, with dignity maybe, and peacefully, but with the same result as any dying. I may still admire him, but I would admire him as a person who *used to be* my friend.

I feel a good deal of melancholy when I think of it, but it is true that we cannot count on mutual admiration to make friendships last forever, any more than we can expect friendships to last because friends like each other or are useful to each other. If friendships like these do happen to last a lifetime, it is probably because they are more than friendships of affection, or usefulness, or admiration. Most likely, they are held together because the friends are committed to each other.

COMMITMENTS GIVE FRIENDSHIPS A LONGER LEASE ON LIFE

We all want *faithful* friends. That is, we want friends who are committed to us. We want the sort of friends who stick with us even when being our friends costs them something.

What sort of commitment is right for friendships? What kind of commitment should we make to our friends?

Recall that we don't usually begin friendship with a commitment. The commitment comes to life gradually. We commit ourselves to each other in snippets, in all sorts of little ways, over a long haul.

We hardly notice when we have first made a commitment to be a friend to someone. But when our friends have special needs, or get into tough situations, we discover that we actually have made a commitment to them without thinking much about it. What sort of commitment is it? I think we make three sorts of commitments, and these are fundamental for lasting friendships.

First, commitment is about loyalty.
We don't betray friends, never treat them the way people

treat enemies: for instance, we don't tell their secrets to other people. And we don't desert them, we don't treat them like strangers even when they are in a lot of trouble.

Dean Acheson, Harry Truman's secretary of state, went to visit his friend Alger Hiss in prison, convicted traitor though Hiss was, bad politics though it was to visit him. When more prudent politicians condemned him publicly, Acheson simply said, "A friend does not forsake a friend just because he is in jail." That's loyalty.

When Richard Nixon was at the lowest ebb of his presidency, at the nadir of Watergate, he got a letter from Harold Macmillan, the former prime minister of England. The letter read, in part, "I feel impelled, in view of our long friendship, to send you a message of sympathy and good will. I trust that these clouds may soon roll away."

When Macmillan died a while later, Richard Nixon wrote a tribute to him in *The Times of London*. Among the things he remembered about the prime minister was his letter of friendship. "What you learn when you fail," Nixon wrote, "is that you hear from your friends." Your *loyal* friends.

Loyalty is the heart and soul of any committed friendship. This is probably why it seems so much more horrible that Jesus was betrayed by a friend than it would have seemed if a stranger had turned him in. So much more monstrous that Caesar was stabbed in the back by his friend Brutus than had he been stabbed by Cassius, whom Caesar did not trust anyway.

Loyalty is the consistency that gives friendship a toughness to survive when it costs a person something to stick with a friend.

Second, commitment is about caring.
Caring for a friend is the heart of commitment.

To care is to invest one's self in a friend's fortune. If I care for you as my friend, whatever happens to you happens to me, when sadness hits you it hits me too, when tragedy wallops you it wallops me, when something terrific happens to you I celebrate no matter where I happen to be. What happens to you matters a lot to me, it concerns me, it makes a genuine difference to my own life. This is what care is about: investment in each other.

Caring is a concerto with infinite variations, but consider two of them.

To care is to make time for friends, interrupt our work schedules, put aside Saturday chores, have breakfast with a friend instead of going to church. We don't have this kind of time to give many friends. And we don't have the energy. Some of us can manage time for only one or two really close friends. Not many of us can do justice to more than three.

To care is to be honest with friends. A friend is not an idol. Nor is a friend an uncritical fan. Friendship cannot survive long on benevolent fakery, nor do friends stay friends for long when one of them uses flattery to win friendship. For friendship to last we need to care enough to be honest. Of course, the caring has to be transparent *in* our honesty; honesty without caring can ruin a friendship. But if we care, we will be honest.

Third, commitment is about accepting a friend's claim on us.

A friend has a right to expect us to do things for her that we would not do for just anyone: give her special consideration, do her special favors, show her special concern, go the extra mile to be with her. And if you ask her, "Why should I?" she has every right to reply, "Just because I'm your friend."

Friends play favorites, the way parents favor their children above their neighbors' children. That's what friendship is about. And they should expect it from each other. They have a claim on it.

I had a best friend once, Cal Bulthuis, the closest friend I have ever had, my friend until he died, and I believe that he would have been my friend until I died, no matter how long I lived.

We met, the way good friends often do, accidentally, in a registration line at Calvin College where he, back from the war, was enrolling as a freshman born out of due time. We both had a hunch, I think, then and there, that we might hit it off.

Our friendship took time to take root, of course, and there were dry spells, but it grew, and we finally became committed friends. We stayed best friends for twenty-five years, until cancer came between us and killed him.

We never said much about our friendship until just before he died.

I had lived in California for three years when he got cancer in his liver that surgeons could not cut away. I called his doctor; he told me that if I wanted to talk with Cal before he died, I should get back to Michigan pretty quickly. So I got on a flight to Grand Rapids the next day, and spent a week with him in his hospital room, talking about a lot of things we had never talked about before.

We talked, for instance, about our friendship.

I told Cal that I was grateful to God that he had been my friend for so long. He told me he was grateful for my friendship too. And we cried.

Then he told me about some things he saw in me that worried him, and that he hoped I would do something about them after he was gone. I promised I would. We cried some more. And we talked about God, and what he thought it would be like when he saw God.

He said that he wished we had talked this way once in a while before, and I said I did too. Once in a while, not often for goodness's sake, but now and then, we agreed, friends ought to speak to each other about their affection. And their cares.

In one way our friendship was in the classic mold: we liked each other, were useful to each other, and admired each other.

It came easy for us. We grew out of the same soil. We were both conscious of being Dutch, and our Dutchness told us a lot about who we were, the way Jews know something important about who they are because they know they are Jewish. We had the same religion: we believed and we doubted the same things. We liked the same sort of women, and books, and movies. So there was a lot about us that each of us knew all about without having to talk about it a lot.

But we percolated all the stuff we shared through different personal filters. He was tidy, I was sloppy. He took forever to do things, I was in a hurry. He felt pretty good about himself, I was forever worried that people would discover that I was a fake. He had an eye for clothes, I wore what I was told to wear. A nice blend. I liked and admired him for the very things that made him different from me. So we were lucky; it was easy for us to be friends.

And yet our friendship lasted because we made a commitment to each other. A thousand commitments, little ones, again and again, as we had occasion to make them.

We never spoke a vow. Never used the word *commitment*.

Grew into it without thinking much about it. But it was a commitment all the same and, like all commitments, had to be renewed regularly.

And I think that to last for any time at all, *any* friendship needs a commitment.

Still, even committed friendship can die. And something in us wants a good friendship to last for life.

This life is worse off when friendship is all ad hoc, relished today, relinquished tomorrow, especially when friendship dies because friends do not care enough.

Maybe our longing for lasting friendship is a hint that heaven must be real. That there must be a time and a place where nobody is just a poor neighbor whom you have to love out of charity. Or because he is family. There must be a place and a time where everyone is a friend to everyone else because everyone likes each other. Where we can all be close friends, where nobody gets closed out of the inner circle.

And where good friendships do not die.

Let's stand back a bit and take another look at where we have been in this chapter.

We do want a friend, a close friend, who stays our friend always. We want a lasting friend as much as we want a lasting lover. Even more, sometimes. But friendship does not seem to be meant to last forever, not when it is blended only of the three classic ingredients: affection, advantage, and admiration. The more reason, then, to remember that commitment is the one thing we can add to ordinary friendship to make it last longer, sometimes for life.

Our hearts tell us that friendship *ought* to last forever. And the longings we have for lasting friendships may be a hint that we are meant for them after all, that the day will come when every good friendship lasts forever.

CHAPTER 7

Why Should a Marriage Be Forever?

President Kennedy's mother, Rose, once decided that she had had enough of life with her high-rolling, woman chasing husband, Joe, and she walked out on him. She was so hurt and so angry that she took the first three of all those children of destiny still to come, went back to her family home, and told Joe she couldn't stand him anymore and wasn't coming back. Her father welcomed her back to the fold. For a couple of months. And then he sent her back to Joe—with these words: "You've made your commitment, Rosie."

What kind of thing was that to say to a troubled daughter who had gotten desperately unhappy with the way her husband was carrying on with other women? Why did Rose Kennedy have to be reminded of a commitment she had made before she had had a solid notion of the sort of man she was marrying? Because it was a lifetime commitment, her father said, for better or for worse. Rose was obedient. She went back to Joe, lived with him until he died, and became a legendary believer in lifetime commitments.

But why *should* she, or we, or anybody, for that matter, ever stick himself or herself with a commitment for life when none of us has a duckling's notion of what is in store?

About four million Americans will make lifetime commitments this year. Most of them will expect to keep their commitments; almost half of them will split before fifteen years are over. The figures dismay a lot of us. But, looking at it another way, maybe we should be impressed that half of them will stick with it through the worst and best of times.

Remember that we are talking about a commitment to the most fragile, the most threatened, of all human relationships. Can any commitment compare with marriage for the pain it can bring? And haven't many of us been converted to the relaxing proposition that "till death us do part" is a nostalgic leftover from a buried antiquity no one will ever see again? So a fifty-percent survival rate may be something about which to crow.

My son Charlie married a splendid woman named Kimberly this past summer. And each of them made a lifetime commitment without batting an eye, serenely sure that nothing, absolutely nothing, could ever get in the way of their love for each other. Guileless children that they were, they swore to stay together and love each other until death put its final quietus on their relationship.

How could they have known what they were getting into? So much can happen later on, so much that they will not be able to control. How could they have known what they were doing on that idyllic night in summer when they promised to cleave to each other through every unidyllic winter? How could they have known how unidyllic some winters can get?

Well, I expect that Charlie and Kim have the stuff to be among the survivors. But the bigger issue still persists: why *should* they have been asked to promise that they would stick together for life?

That's what we are going to think about in this chapter: *why*? Does a lifetime commitment to anyone really make sense today? Why not a six-month commitment, with an option to renew, or a commitment to a two-year trial? Why should we start out with a promise to make it last forever?

There are, after all, plausible reasons for *not* making lifetime commitments. I can think of three reasons for keeping all commitments open-ended, just in case. Here they are, the three of them, condensed.

WE CHANGE AFTER WE MAKE COMMITMENTS

Sometimes we change a lot, and two married people do not always change in the same ways or at the same pace.

"I have grown a lot since we've been married, but Jean just hasn't kept up. Now she is holding me back. I know that she has to grow at the pace she thinks is right for her. But we cannot grow together anymore; we can only grow apart. So the decent thing for me to do is leave her."

Or turn the page. "Joan has changed so much I hardly recognize her as the person I married. Back then she really wanted to care for me and the kids, but now she doesn't want us to get in the way of her career. I don't know her anymore. She certainly isn't the person I promised to live with."

EVERYONE HAS A RIGHT TO REPAIR MISTAKES

We all try to cut our losses when we realize we have put our money in the wrong mutual fund. We switch jobs when we have reached a dead end in our career. We change from Baptist to Presbyterian when we find a friendlier church in our new neighborhood. We trade in our car when we have a lemon on our hands. So that venerable sociologist Margaret Mead asks in her book *Male and Female:* "If past mistakes are to be repairable in every other field of human relationships, why should marriage be the exception?" Well, why should it?

EVERYONE HAS A RIGHT TO STOP POINTLESS PAIN

Nobody on this earth has a right to perfect happiness. But surely we have a right to put a stop to pointless pain. If Pam's putting up with painful stuff from Paul, her angry husband, is not doing either of them any good, and is in fact doing them both a lot of harm, their pain has no purpose. It isn't leading them anywhere as persons, and it is killing their happiness and their marriage. So if Pam cannot get Paul to quit hurting her, it simply isn't fair to expect her to put up with a brutal husband just for the sake of her commitment.

So we have three reasons for taking the "fatal forever" out of commitment to marriage.

The chips are down: is it still reasonable to make a *lifetime* commitment to marriage and to keep it in the face of these plausible arguments for keeping our bags packed, just in case?

I should tell you at this point what lifetime commitment is

about. It is not about length of time, not first of all, not basically. I don't, for example, think along these lines: "If I live for another 20 years, I will have to live with Doris for 240 months, or 1,040 weeks. Can I stick with her for that long?" I don't think about the calendar when I think about my commitment. Nor do people I know. Not the ones who are committed. It's when we are not committed that we worry about the number of years ahead of us.

Committed people don't hunker down before the terrors and tedium of time to come. In fact, many of us make our commitments by the day. We choose each day to put someone else's needs ahead of our wishes. We choose each day to care for someone.

Then what does the lifetime in commitment mean?

Lifetime means "unconditional."

A lifetime commitment is about not having exit routes along the way, just in case things don't work out the way we had expected. For instance, a lifetime commitment would never sound like this: "I'll stay with you unless you get stomach cancer." Or "I'll be with you as long as you remain thin." Or "I'll stick with you until somebody better comes along." A lifetime commitment doesn't have escape clauses in the fine print.

So lifetime commitments are simply commitments we intend to keep, no matter what.

Most of us seem to believe that marriage entails this sort of commitment because of the sort of thing marriage is. For instance, we still *get* married only when we are ready for commitment.

Isn't this why we need ceremonies? Let it be a high sacrament in a sacred chapel or a flat formality in a civil chamber, we want a ceremony of some sort. The reason we need a ceremony is that we want to make vows for everyone to hear, vows to live together until the sharp blade of death slices us apart, vows spoken in a festive setting, vows we celebrate afterward with our friends and family.

Someone asked Jane why she and Rick did not get married; after all they had been living together for a couple of years and they seemed to hit it off well.

This was Jane's answer: "We are not sure we are ready to make the commitment. The way things are now, Rick is free to go whenever he wants to go, and so am I, and we want to be able to split without any guilt-soaked fuss about breaking a commitment. When we are ready to make the commitment to each other, we will get married."

Jane senses a difference between a choice to live together for the time being and a commitment to stick together no matter what. So do most people.

But *why* does it make such sense to us?

The reason must lie with deep human needs that we all share, needs intimately tied to marriage, needs that only a lifetime commitment can meet.

What we need most is *trust*.

There is probably no other person in the world we need to trust so much as we need to trust the person we marry. And nothing creates trust like knowing that the other person is unconditionally committed. Legalities do not help much. Would it help, when we felt specially insecure, if our partner said: "You've got a marriage license, isn't that enough for you?" Would it help if our partner offered us a contract that guaranteed us a fair share of things in the event that he—or she—should leave us? Not really.

It takes a personal commitment to create trust. Not just a vow spoken a year, ten years, a lifetime, ago. But a commitment reborn every day by our reliable presence, renewed by acts of care, resurrected by generous forgiving. Our commitment to someone in caring love is the only guarantee we can give, the only basis for trust.

But why do we *need* to trust each other so completely?

Let me count some ways. There are probably more, but here are some needs that I sense and I mention them because they seem to be universal.

WE NEED TO TRUST EACH OTHER WITH OUR GIFT

We need to trust each other so much because we *give* each other so much. Think of commitment as a gift—the gift of one self to another. Quite a gift! The Swiss psychologist Paul Tournier talks of it this way in his book *The Meaning of Gifts*. "The 'I do' is a gift," he said, "total, definite, unreserved . . . a personal and unchangeable commitment." Quite a commitment!

We give a big chunk of ourselves, the most vulnerable part, the part that gets hurt badly if it is let down or betrayed. And trust is the only way we have of coping with the risk of such extravagant giving.

Maybe the supreme moment, or at least the most sensitive symbol, of giving and trusting is the moment of making love. At least if there is passion in it (which is certainly not always the case). But when we do *give* love as well as *make* love, we give a gift that we cannot take back again. And giving it leaves us exposed, open to joy and open to pain. The sadness of being left alone after we have given such a sensitive part of ourself away can be chilling. How we need to trust each other with our gift!

It's something like the way we once trusted our mother. We become like the children we were when we trusted our mother to stay with us, to give us her tender touch and her soothing hum, to come back again whenever she left us, to be with us even when she would rather be somewhere else.

WE NEED TO TRUST SOMEONE TO CARE FOR US

We need to trust someone to care for us during the low ebbs, when life's energy bottoms out, and we are too weak, too tired, to take care of ourself. We need to be able to trust another to care for us when we fall down and can't get up by ourselves, when we cry out for help, when we make bad mistakes, when we are afraid. Within us all beats the heart of a needy child. So we need a commitment that sets no advance limits to caring.

Care and consistency are point and counterpoint in the music of marriage. They are played in a delicate duet of mutual need. And we have got to be forever improvising on the score of who cares for whom and who is cared for at any given moment of need. Each of the players trusts the other to move in to take up the slack when one of them misses a beat.

Living out of commitment is more like New Orleans jazz than a classical Haydn piece. It is improvising on a theme called promise. If we can't improvise we have a bad problem.

When we care deeply for each other, we gradually get linked into each other's lives, woven into each other's being. We may love each other with mild and, once in a while, if we are lucky, with wild, desire, and even hate each other for a little while. But we keep on improvising new ways of caring through the undertow of passion and the overflow of commitment.

Our need for caring does not stop; we never outgrow it. So when two weak and needy and flawed persons share their lives, they need a commitment that does not have any options for quitting whenever one person requires too much care.

I've been saying that we have two basic human needs that make a lifetime commitment crucial to a marriage. We need to trust someone with our gift. We need to trust someone to care for us. Now we must think about the needs that a third party has for both of us.

OUR CHILDREN NEED TO TRUST US

Our fathers and mothers had a hunch that a marriage wasn't complete without children for whom to care. Something in me feels that they had a point.

I became tuned in to my own feelings about this when Doris and I decided to adopt our three children.

Why did we do it? I'll tell you why *I* think we did it: I think we were following an impulse we couldn't resist, an inner nudge to give our marriage a deeper meaning than we could give it by ourselves. The gift of love we gave each other motivated us to want to give the gift of life to others. And adoption was the closest thing we could come to it.

We were not being noble at all, as if we were giving these three kids a break. We knew that. And, to be honest, we didn't offer them that great a deal anyway; there were other couples waiting to adopt children, and they might have been better parents for them than we were. Anyway, we adopted them for our own sakes. I remember overhearing a silly woman telling my teenage daughter that it was very nice of her parents to have adopted her. Cathy, more cocky than sassy, came back: "I don't think so; I think they were just lucky." She was pretty close to the truth.

Children are one reason why a commitment to a spouse is different from a commitment to a friend. Commit yourself to a friend, and you make a promise to a single person. Commit yourself to a husband or a wife, and you are making a com-

mitment to your children too. To the third and fourth genera-
tions. They are grafted into our commitment; they have their
own claim on the commitment we make to each other.

Our children are not waiting in line for a free ticket into our
marriage, they don't knock on our door and beg to be part of
the deal. We sneak them inside of our commitment to each other
without consulting their preferences. We tuck them inside of our
own coupling. And when we do, we endow them with an inalienable right to have us both around as long as they need us.

Children get anxious if they so much as wonder much
whether their parents really intend to stick together. They feel
double-crossed if their parents actually leave each other. When
two parents cannot keep the commitment they once made to
each other, they fail a commitment to the kids. And it hurts
them; there seems to be no way of getting around it.

I will take a cue from what psychologist Archibald Hart says
in his book *Children of Divorce,* and run through some of the hurt
most children feel when their parents get a divorce.

GRIEF: When children lose one of their parents to a divorce,
they feel it the way a parent feels a death in the family.

CONFLICT: When children are forced to choose between two
people they need, they feel caught and wounded in the conflict.

FEAR: When children feel their secure family structure trembling like a bridge in an earthquake, they tremble too, for
fear of what will happen to them next.

GUILT: When their parents can't stay together, their children
have a guilty hunch that it is their fault.

DEPRESSION: When children lose someone they need to fill out
the meaning of their lives, they are programmed for depression.

Enough. It isn't the end of the world for children of divorce.
They are not damned to some inferior status ever after. They
usually survive and often succeed, but their resilience does not
take away the hurt when it happens. It is a blow. No child who
feels it ever deserves it, and none forgets it.

So when we ask why unconditional commitment still makes
sense for marriage, children are part of the answer. A commit-

ment to each other is a promise to them. They have a right to trust us to keep it.

OUR COMMUNITY NEEDS TO TRUST US

Each of us needs a community of people to be supported by. We can't make it hanging on the thin, quivering branch of our individual, lonely existence. But a human community is a delicate web that is knit together with the invisible thread of personal commitments.

It isn't our laws, or our licenses, or our contracts that keep a community human. We need these legalities to hold each other accountable. We need them in our political and business organizations. But they are only supports we contrive to strengthen the network of personal commitments.

Real community, a sharing, caring community, is created by the trust we have in each other's personal promises. The trust we have in the free commitments we make to each other—with or without contracts.

The stronger our personal commitments are, the stronger the whole community is. If too many of us renege on our personal commitments, we weaken the web that holds a society together.

Marriage is one of the pivotal commitments in any community. When a lot of marriages break up, especially if a family is broken too, the thread of the web wears thin.

So our communities need to trust people to make lifetime commitments and to keep them.

The sum and substance of this chapter comes down to this: we have a deep need to trust each other when we get married, and our need for trust is why a lifetime commitment is right for marriage. Not easy. But right.

We need to trust each other because we give each other so much. We need to trust each other because we have a need to be cared for; we have a child inside of us that never grows out of this need. And the children we are committed to care for have a need—even a right—to trust us to stay together. Our community needs to trust us to stay together; and because we have no life except life in community, our community has a right to trust us too.

Our many-sided need to trust each other shows us the point of lifetime commitments, commitments without conditions, commitments without escape clauses.

But it is one thing to say that marriage needs a lifetime commitment, and quite another to assume that everyone can make good on that commitment, or even should. We must talk about this in the next chapter.

CHAPTER 8

When a Marriage Cannot Be Forever

When a young Rose Kennedy had had her bellyfull of Joe's playing around with other women and wanted to leave him, her
father told her she couldn't go back on a lifetime commitment:
it was forever.

Many years later Rose's daughter Kathleen fell in love with
a divorced Englishman, Lord Peter Fitzwilliam, and wanted to
marry him. But, when she heard about it, Rose Kennedy's deepest beliefs took hold of her. If you marry this man, she told
Kathleen, you will be cast out of the Kennedy family, disowned,
regarded as dead. Not long afterward a private plane Kathleen
and Peter were flying in crashed into a German mountain and
both died.

Why did Rose Kennedy treat her own daughter so cruelly,
Kathleen, the favorite sister of all the Kennedy women, she who
had already lost a husband to the war?

The reason was that Rose's father had taught her that Lord
Peter was still married to his ex-wife, that if Kathleen married
Lord Peter, she would be marrying a married man. Rose believed
that once a person made a lifetime commitment to marriage, that
person is married forever.

Rose believed that there was no exit from marriage. She believed, just as many other people have believed, that marriage
was a kind of invisible house that two people got locked into
whenever they were properly wed. They were wedlocked inside
the holy estate of matrimony. This is what Rose Kennedy be-

lieved; it was a belief that gave her the courage to stick with her husband and made her capable of disowning her daughter.

The status of divorced people, in this view, is something like the status of escaped convicts. Prisoners on the run may walk around town as if they were free people, but they are convicts in the "eyes of the law." Divorced people may walk around as if they were free of each other, but they are still wedlocked in the "eyes of God." If we are married forever in the eyes of God, there is no escape from our commitment. Once in, always in.

My problem with this theory of marriage is that it does not make sense.

When two people determine to leave each other for good, and get a court to declare them unmarried in the eyes of the law, their marriage is dead and gone, a memory, a sad memory perhaps, but only a memory, nothing more. Any marriage can die. We may with all our hearts intend it to last for life. And we may believe that it should last for life. But it can die. There are exits.

Now let's look at marriage commitment from another point of view, one that puts up exit signs wherever we may want to get off. This view lies at the other end of the world from all that Rose Kennedy believes about commitment to marriage. We pick it up in what Ralph Karsten learned from his therapist.

Two months after he got a divorce, Ralph was walloped by remorse for having failed to keep his commitment. In the old days he would have gone to a minister with his problem, maybe for help in seeking forgiveness. But being a thoroughly modern person, Ralph went to an expensive therapist in Santa Barbara to seek a cure.

This is what his therapist told him: you should be grateful. You have completed an important stage on your journey of self-discovery. Your ex-wife has traveled with you up to this point, and she has helped you along as far as she has been able to go with you. So be thankful for her gift, and take it with you as you leave. If she has any style at all, she will return the compliment.

Ralph's therapist made good sense—given her idea of what a commitment to marriage was all about.

For her, a person's commitment to marriage is an investment

in his or her own growth. Growth, that is, toward the happier, the better, the more satisfied, person he or she is capable of becoming. It stands to reason, then, that when a person's investment in a relationship has not yielded any growth for a while, it's time to get out of it, and to seek another relationship with greater potential for personal profit.

Looked at this way, a marriage commitment is an intimate version of "Let's Make a Deal." There is something in it for you, something in it for me. When there is not enough in it for either one of us, one of us should call the deal off. No hard feelings.

Exits from commitment? You can find one at every intersection of your marriage. Whenever you get low on growth, it's time to look for one.

The "growth for me" theory of commitment is businesslike, hard-nosed practical, therapeutic—and eminently self-centered. My problem with this theory is that when it is put into practice, it stifles real growth.

Real growth is healthiest when we put commitment to another person ahead of growth for ourself. There is such a thing as growing into maturity, becoming strong enough to stick with a relationship because we care about the other person too much to leave it. And maybe we grow a notch too, when we learn to accommodate ourself to the fact that no relationship brings us everything we want.

The right planter's mix for personal growth is a blend of realism with commitment. We don't grow into mature persons by chasing fantasies. And one fact about marriage in general is that every marriage in particular is imperfect. No one marries exactly the right person; we all marry someone who is only more or less right for us. We are all flawed partners. And if we accept this regrettable but invigorating fact of life, we may be ready for real growth.

We do not give ourself a good chance for growing personally if we keep hankering after our fantasy of the ideal woman. Or man. We grow when we keep renewing our commitment to the only spouse we've got. We grow when we stop dreaming of a perfect marriage, and adjust caringly to the one we have. Our best growth comes when we forget about our own growth, and focus on caring instead.

Here's a nice twist: instead of giving us a good reason for giving up a lifetime commitment, our need to grow is a prime reason for keeping it.

Let's recapitulate. Rose Kennedy believed in lifetime commitment, but she closed her eyes to the reality that sometimes we need an exit from commitment. Ralph's therapist saw exits anywhere we want to leave. But she did not believe in lifetime commitment.

Common sense lands us in the middle.

I gave some reasons in chapter seven why lifetime commitments still make sense for marriage. Now I must say that it makes sense, sad sense, but real sense, to say that some people who make a life commitment cannot keep it for life. There must be an exit for them.

When is it right to exit from commitment? I'll put some possibilities on the table, and we can discuss them in turn.

WHEN IS IT NOT POSSIBLE TO KEEP A COMMITMENT?

Ask Becky why she finally cut loose and left Frank after sticking with him for fifteen years. She will tell you that she left because it was *impossible* for her to stay. She *had* to go.

It became obvious about a dozen years ago that Frank was an alcoholic; he needed help, but raged like a lanced bull whenever Becky or anyone else urged him to get it. Frank was not an amiable drunk: he ravaged Becky with hate when he was in his cups, whipped her with barbed words and, now and then, when the torrent of his rage broke the dam of his fears, with bare hands. Had she stayed, her life, like her love, would have been as good as finished.

One way to look at it is that Becky did not go back on commitment when she left Frank. She came to the conclusion that Frank had killed her commitment by making it impossible for her to keep it.

Other people feel choked within a marriage to a fine person who would kill himself or herself before abusing the other. Their partners are not cruel, or unfaithful, or insane. It's just that their two characters are so dreadfully incompatible with each other that one or both of them feel smothered by the combination.

Karen, a friend of mine, still admires the man she divorced

a couple of years ago. He is generous, faithful, and has all sorts of other moral qualities that she was taught to admire in a person. But, as she tells it and as she feels it, he doesn't have what she needs most. He doesn't have the power to communicate care for her in a message she can hear. He stays detached and gives her the feeling a spy must get when she is caught and her government washes its hands of her, leaves her out in the cold with no hope that anybody will be in touch.

Maybe it's partly her own doing; maybe she doesn't have the ears to hear what he really wants her to hear or the eyes to see what he wants her to see. I don't know. Nobody knows, except her. And I can't be sure that even she knows. But when I ask her why she doesn't go back to him, she says, "To go back to that marriage would kill me."

Somehow, for her, it was impossible to keep her commitment even though when she made it she meant with all her heart to keep it.

Everything I believe about commitment wants me to remind Karen that people give up hope too soon, see their problems too quickly as catastrophes. I want to talk to her about hope, because I suspect she decided too soon that staying was impossible.

But I also believe Karen when she tells me that *for her* it is not possible to keep the commitment she made and meant for life.

WHEN DOES KEEPING A COMMITMENT LOSE ITS POINT?

Ask Bruce why he is getting a divorce from Samantha.

He will tell you that his marriage has *lost its point*.

No point in staying, he says, when the point of staying is gone. True? Consider his story and decide for yourself.

Samantha was a religious lady, sober as a nun, and just about as chaste. She was committed to decency, even as her mother was before her; she loved decency perhaps more than life, certainly more than love, and as her decency heated up her passion cooled down.

She thought she was chaste, but what she really was was mean. She could take a bead on Bruce's soul, smack him with her contempt, and slice him apart the way a fisherman fillets a halibut. To her, Bruce's gift of passion was only a male's disguise for animal lust. And she made him understand quite clearly that she was not willing to be sacrificed on the pagan altar of his degraded desires.

For Bruce, keeping commitment was a long-term lease on humiliation. He felt like a puppy being spanked for being in heat. Keeping commitment became a euphemism for dying alone on the dry sands of Samantha's savage decency.

Samantha claimed that she was committed. But she had only one-half of the equation. She had consistency but no care. She was predictable but refused to be present. And sometimes half a commitment is worse than no commitment at all.

Was there any point in keeping it? Did Bruce's commitment have any point when Samantha rejected his gift of sexual love and could not give him the gift of care?

Let's admit it: a lifetime commitment to stay together "no matter what" can run up against some conditions that make keeping it impossible or, if not impossible, then pointless. In a world where married people can abuse each other, demean each other, be disloyal to each other, and be generally destructive to each other and their children, it is not realistic to assume that everyone who makes a lifetime commitment can keep it for life.

WHEN DO WE KNOW WE MADE AN UNWISE CHOICE?

A lifetime commitment is often scuttled at the launching because we are not smart about the person to whom we make it. A person doesn't release himself or herself from a lifetime commitment simply because he or she has no grit, no fidelity, no character. People often leave a commitment because the person they made a commitment to was the sort of person doomed to be trouble.

I said before that we don't know what we are doing when we make a lifetime commitment. It is just as true that few of us know *who we really are* when we make one. Or who the other person is.

Two people fall in love. Crazily, wondrously, insanely, beautifully. Blind to who each other really is. How can they know? They are lunatics—for the time being.

They come from different schools of life. They have different parents, had different childhoods. They have developed different levels of tolerance to pain. They have different religions and different morals, different ways of coping with disappointment, different talents for hurting each other, different sets of neuroses.

The message in all this is that we need to be wiser, more careful, more understanding, when making a lifetime commitment.

My friend Neil Warren, a psychologist with twenty-five years' experience in counseling people whose commitments are in trouble, gave me a list of the most common mistakes people make when they make lifetime commitments:

They commit too quickly.
They commit before they are mature.
They have unrealistic expectations.
They commit while drunk on romantic love.
They have a wretched self-image.
They don't know how to communicate.
They don't share the same faith or values.

Unwise choice, dubious commitment. We do make commitment keeping hard for ourselves later by the choices we make earlier. In fact, we can make it next to impossible in the end by making bad commitments at the start.

But there is something else worth thinking about: a mistake at the start does not *have* to mean failure at the finish.

None of us marries the one perfect person for us; to be honest, there is no such person. But most of us can accommodate ourselves to the less-than-perfect person we did marry, even if we were not seeing straight when we married him—or her.

Often when two people decide that they married the wrong person, they are really refusing to let each other be the special individuals they are. They hold the thoroughly wrongheaded notion that two committed people ought to be totally alike. And they also believe that if people remain very different from each other, they have cause to split.

When I think of people I know who have not only kept their commitment, but who have developed an unusually good relationship over the years, my mind gets a fix on two friends who are as different from one another as two people could possibly be. He is spiritual; she is earthy. He is detached; she loves to be intimate with people. He is dependent; she could manage almost anything by herself. He is offended by vulgarity; she laughs at anything that is funny. He is always careful; she likes to take risks. He sees life in blacks and whites; she embraces all the grays and shadows of life. He hates conflict; she dares take on anyone. They are very different.

What has kept their commitment alive in spite of all the stress of their differences? It has been the creative power of the care they have nourished for each other even when their differences have pushed them apart.

But they do not choke each other with care. Just the opposite. They care by giving each other permission to be the different sort of person each of them is. They care enough to leave each other alone, enough to celebrate the gifts each brings within his or her character. These two people have turned commitment into joy, mostly because they have gradually learned how to set each other free.

It took me too long to discover the difference between *active* caring and *permissive* caring. In active caring we do things to help someone. In permissive caring we let people be who they are and do what they need to do.

Active caring was easy for me. I was prepared to *do* just about anything for Doris. In anybody's league I was a devoted husband. If she went away for a few days, I would clean the oven for her while she was gone because I knew she hated the job. But there was a cheap, selfish hook in this kind of caring. I was really proving to myself—and to her—that I was a caring husband. An ancient gambit, boring, and silly, too.

But in my heart I failed at the most critical challenge of caring—giving Doris permission to be who she was, and permission to give me the gifts that she had to give. She had a lighthearted gift for smelling the roses, whenever and wherever she found them, even if it meant putting off some chores. I had a gift of plowing through obstacles and getting things done, quickly, now.

I thought, early on, that I had a calling to convert Doris to my kind of work ethic. But my missionary efforts made us both miserable. Then she gradually taught me the secret of permissive caring—the toughest kind of caring for a work-obsessed person such as myself. But as I learned the freedom of permissive caring, I was ready for a more interesting partnership between two very different sorts of characters.

Permissive caring is one way of living with the fact that we chose the wrong person. A creative way. It is the way of permitting our partner to be the very person we didn't know we were marrying. And of discovering that what looks like incompatibility can become a duet of differences.

I do not mean to say, of course, that everyone who makes a bad choice of commitment can survive the original mistake. Sometimes living together is destructive as, for instance, when one person is incurably brutal. In that case the sooner the commitment is undone the better.

HOW DO WE KNOW IF IT'S RIGHT TO QUIT?

My friends ask me, if there are times to quit, how do we know if our time has come? How do we know when it is right to leave our commitment? When it has become impossible to go on? When going on has lost its point? How do we know?

My answer is, If our hearts are right, we will know.

Ah, our hearts, yes, but our hearts pull the wool over our eyes. We cannot count on our hearts; our hearts are sneaky things.

And yet they are the best we have. So the important thing is to keep them tuned to caring.

To begin with, we could change the mood of the question, make it more positive. Instead of asking how we know when we cannot keep our commitment any longer, we could ask how we know that we should keep on trying.

One thing that helps is to get close to honest people who have faced up to and worked through tougher problems than ours, close enough so that we can see into their secrets for successful caring and coping.

It's a little like knowing how to tell great art from fakery; if you look at real art often enough, you will see the difference, and your heart will not trick you. In the same way, if we know enough people who have learned to swim together through seas of trouble, we will have a better eye for hints of possibilities within our own troubled waters.

But if we are to learn by looking at examples of the art of

commitment keeping, we need people around us who will let us look into their lives and see the truth about them.

We need to get inside a community of real people, honest people, who are willing to let us see how they struggled against the odds to keep their commitments. Who keep struggling because they keep hope alive together. And who keep hope alive because they keep on caring enough to want to be hopeful. Or people too who were once defeated, divorced, and are now doing better at it the second time. Our hearts learn the truth from honest strugglers who dare to open the windows of their lives to us.

The trick is to find a real community, not an insider's club. Not a group that makes believe it is a community just because everyone recites the same creed. But a community where people care enough to give each other permission to be strugglers, wounded strugglers, who are hanging on to their commitments by their fingernails. A community that cares enough to permit people to fail helps people dare to reveal their own struggles, including their failures as well as successes.

I don't mean a group where people at their fortieth anniversary muse—in a fuzzy, nostalgic way—that it has not always been easy for them to achieve their graying bliss. I mean a group in which people dare to talk in the present tense, and say something like, "Jane and I are having a very devil of a time of it these days, and we're not sure we can stay together, but we don't want to quit trying, not yet." I mean a community in which strugglers dare to ask other strugglers how they are doing it.

If we are going to help each other in the challenge of commitment keeping, we will have to risk being transparent to each other. The only people who were ever truly helpful to Doris and me were the ones who let us see and feel the inside story of their struggles, including their defeats and their compromises, and how they turned commitment keeping into an adventure of imperfect, but caring, love. They helped us in two ways: first, by giving us hope that, if they could make it, so could we; and second, by letting us know that we were not alone in our efforts to turn commitment keeping into creative partnership.

In short, one way to explore the possibilities that our situation is not as hopeless as we may think it is, is to get into a community of commitment keepers. An honest community. A transparent community. Only a community of transparent strugglers can keep our hearts honest when we wonder whether the time has come to fold our cards and walk away from commitment.

A simple summary of this chapter will do: commitment to marriage is meant to be forever, but what is meant to be cannot always be. Not in the real world of weak and needy and faulty folk.

Unconditional commitments can be undone by incurable conditions. We weave the tapestry of our commitments with the threads of our wobbly wills. And in this vale of vile winds, our most beautiful tapestries can be torn to shreds. We are all flawed people trying to keep our commitments to flawed people. And sometimes it gets too much for some of us.

The more reason, then, to remember that when we want to know where we are going, it helps to go back to where we began. Back to commitment—to the hopeful proposition that, with care, we may be able to make things better than they are, good enough to put up with, at least, and maybe even good enough to translate the rigors of commitment into a modest harvest of happiness.

CHAPTER 9

The Promises We Make
to Our Children

Fred Fergusen is getting along in years, is a father of three fine grown-up children, and has a lot of reasons to feel good about the job he did fathering them. But every now and then he gets smitten by a notion that he has let his children down.

It is hard for him to put his finger on what it was he failed at. He remembers moments when he lost his temper, like the time in the station wagon, after a long, hot day of driving: he couldn't find the camping site where the Auto Club map said one was supposed to be, the kids got silly and he blew up. Mostly, though, he just remembers personal qualities he didn't have, and wished he had had, like a sense of humor, or more patience and understanding, or enough character to inspire his children to look up to him and want to be like him.

He knows his feelings are out of line with reality. Whatever it was he failed at, his failures look like the marks of ordinary humanity, and they could not have hurt his children much. All three of them are really doing OK, not stars, but responsible adults, plowing their own furrows through the fields they either chose for themselves or drifted into, holding down steady jobs and, all in all, doing all right at being decent human beings in a world that is not as decent as they.

And yet he has this stubborn sense that he failed to keep his commitment to the people in his life who needed him most.

I think I can understand Fred, because I have had the same feelings he has, unspecific, blurred disquiet at not having done as good a job at being a father as I ought to have done. Other parents tell me they have the same feelings. In fact, the more serious they are about their commitment to their children, the harder they seem to judge themselves. Not much wonder either; taking on the job of bringing up children is a huge, lumpy commitment that has few precise terms. How could we expect to feel sure we have kept our commitment well?

So the object of this chapter is to put parental commitment into simple, elemental terms: what kind of commitment *does* a parent make to a child?

I am not talking about the promises that some privileged parents make to their privileged children. College tuition in the bank by the time the child is seventeen. A trust fund, divided equally. A nice spot in the family business. These are options; you can choose them if you happen to be well enough off to commit yourself to them.

I am talking about the commitment that comes as standard equipment with parenting. The kind that matches the job description that comes with taking a child into our care and calling her—or him—our own, no matter how the child happens to arrive. I will be unwrapping, one by one, the essential components of commitments we make to our children. The first three components lie in the minds and hearts of the parents who make the commitment. Then come five things that parents commit themselves to *do* for their children.

COMMITMENTS PARENTS MAKE ARE UNCONDITIONAL

People inside the family circle make unconditional commitments to be there for each other, no matter what.

I am talking about a real family. I am not talking about the family feeling that managers whip up at the office. The way they do, for instance, at Delta Airlines, where the Delta Family Feeling is a corporate slogan meant to stimulate a chummy attitude among the people who work there.

In her book *Divorcing the Corporation*, Jacqueline Plumez cites managers of Fortune 500 companies as saying things such as this: "I love my company. They are the family I turn to when I'm in trouble." And she notes that one of the keys to getting on Fortune's list of the One Hundred Best Companies to Work For is to "make people feel that they are part of a . . . family."

It is a good thing when corporations treat employees like real people who don't leave their souls in the employees parking lot. And it is true that some people get more caring consideration at the job than they do at home. But when Plumez tells us that "the corporation has become the family to the 1980s," I begin to worry.

The quickest way to tell the difference between the boss at Delta and a parent at home is to imagine this scenario. A man gets a form letter telling him that his services to the family are no longer needed. Good-bye, enjoy your severance pay. But he takes the letter to his supervisor and tearfully whines "You can't do this to me; I'm family." The supervisor pats him on the shoulder in fatherly fashion, but answers, "No, you *used* to be family. Now you are fired."

In committed families nobody gets fired.

Mothers and fathers cannot unparent themselves. Not the way a husband can unhusband himself. Or the way a friend can stop being a friend. A father may chuck his daughter out of the house, he might dispossess a child of an inheritance, he can refuse to accept phone calls from a wandering rebel. But he cannot make the child into a nonchild of his. The bonding is permanent. And the commitment is meant to match.

Not everyone who helps to make a child can make a parent's commitment. Now and then two people are led by tragic necessity to allow other people to make the commitment, to be the parents of their child. Real life does not always fit the mold of nature. But the exception only highlights the basic reality about every family: a family is created when a commitment is made, not when a baby is born.

Blood does not make a family. Nobody in my immediate family is blood kin to any of the others. But we are a family. It is unconditional commitment that turns us into a family.

What do I mean by *unconditional?*

I mean that no child needs to meet a certain standard to qualify for his parent's commitment. When a new parent says to a baby, "I am the person who will be there for you," there is no fine print that qualifies the promise. No committed parent ever says, "I'll be there for you as long as you measure up to my expectations." When we accept a child as ours, we say, in effect, "Nothing you could ever do and nothing you could ever become could disqualify you from my commitment."

There is no other commitment like this one for unconditionality. It is truly a "no matter what" relationship, as close to God's commitment as we can get—and what a gift it is!

I remember when Doris's doctor stung us with the prognosis that the baby she was going to deliver in a couple of hours would be very seriously malformed. How badly? Very badly, that's all he could say. During the hours of her labor, Doris and I prodded our hearts to see what courage we could awaken there for unconditional commitment to our grossly handicapped child.

I was not sure of my heart. I needed Doris's courage to cover my fears. But together we promised, then and there, that the child could not be too handicapped for us to make and keep our commitment to him or her. Our promise was unconditional.

As things turned out, it was a boy child, and to our numb joy he was born quite miraculously with all his pieces in place. Then he quite unmiraculously died before we had a chance to test our courage for unconditional commitment keeping. But we knew we had made a "no matter what" kind of commitment, and we knew we could make it again if we had to. And knowing how afraid I was when we made it, I can feel the fears some parents must feel when they commit themselves unconditionally to their children.

The "no matter what" clause provides every child with blanket coverage. No deductibles. No matter if he is genetically unlucky. No matter that she is destined to be a pain in the neck. No matter that the best of parents sometimes end up murmuring that their children are not exactly what they had in mind when they prayed for some fruit from the family tree.

Our daughters may choose values we despise and may despise values we cherish. Our sons may worship strange deities, of whom we have never heard. They may fail at most things they try or not try much of anything. One may fall deep into depression and one may fly high on drugs. We may almost die of fear for them, choke on our anger at them, weep at the pain they suffer, and go broke trying to pay their way.

No matter. Our commitment is for the kind of forever that gives a child permanent membership in our caring ensemble of people we call a family.

COMMITMENTS PARENTS MAKE PUT THEM IN CONTROL

No other commitment we ever make to another person gives us such control over the person to whom we make it. Mostly, when we make commitments to other people, our friends, for instance, they return the compliment. They freely join us in whatever relationship our commitment creates for us. Freely we commit to them, freely they commit to us. Not so when we commit ourselves to be parents to a child; parents do all the committing and they have all the control.

Children never have a chance to vote on the commitment we offer. They cannot even ask for arbitration. No child can say, "No thanks, I'll pass on these two; I'd rather wait for a couple of smarter people, with a better genetic bank account, and richer too, better equipped all around to provide me with the privileges to which I will easily grow accustomed." A child has no choice in the matter. We simply sneak our commitment into their lives, and stick them with us forever more. What control!

Doris and I got a phone call one fine April morning from a social worker named Margaret at an adoption agency named Bethany Home, after the place, I've always assumed, where Mary and Martha opened their home to their friend Jesus. She and her staff had earlier spent weeks giving our credentials for parenthood a thorough going over, and they finally found us adequate. Then they told us we would have to wait for "our" child to turn up. That Friday morning we learned that she had arrived.

So we found her, face puffed like a red melon, bawling, hurting from a scarlet sore on her arm, the mark of a vaccination they had given her the day before, and we committed ourselves to her, on the spot, unconditionally.

She was plunked then and there into a family she did not know, had not chosen, may not have wanted. When we made that commitment to her, we decided what her name would be. We decided where she would live, and thus who her friends would be. Our faith determined the God she would be taught to worship. We selected her grandparents, along with a slew of aunts and uncles and cousins. And, most of all, we decided who would fence her in, every day, hour by hour, with their care—their confining, their bothersome, their loving, their parenting care.

She never had a chance.

It is not meant to last, of course, this control, tempting as it is to hold onto it. The very purpose of all this control is to prepare our children to fly away. But all the same, the chain reaction of our early control dogs their heels for life. And no child ever gets over it completely.

COMMITMENTS PARENTS MAKE ARE SELF-INTERESTED

Parents tend to congratulate themselves, maybe pity themselves, for their committed love, as if a parent's commitment were pure self-giving devotion. But it isn't. We slip a goodly dose of self-serving into our caring commitment.

We sang a gospel song at a missionary Sunday school I was sent to on Sabbath afternoons that put these words in God's mouth:

> I gave, I gave my life for thee.
> What hast thou given for me, for me?
> I gave, I gave my life for thee.
> What hast thou given for me?

It was about God's commitment to us. But it made us feel that God might have been asking too much in return, wanting more from us than we could give. How could we ever pay him back? Can anyone ever get even with God?

Some parents have their own version of the gospel song:

> I gave, I gave the best years of my life for thee.
> What have you given to me, to me,
> What have you given to me?
> Not even a phone call!

The tone of it is, when parents commit themselves to their children, they give and give and give, all for their kids, only for them. Why can't they see how much they owe us?

But in our hearts we know the truth.

We know that when we make our commitments to our children, we expect a good return on our investment. By the time we hold the red, wrinkled creature in our arms, we are dreaming dreams we know will make us happy. And some of us let them know too soon and too often that we don't want to be disappointed.

Now and then, seduced by pious illusion, I have persuaded myself that Doris and I adopted our dear children for their sakes. Who am I kidding? What we were doing was what every parent on God's procreative planet does: we were following an inner nudge to give our marriage, and our lives, a deeper meaning and richer love than we could give it by ourselves.

It was not that big a break for them anyway; there were plenty of couples with the same needs we had, waiting in the wings and, who knows, they might have suited our children better than we did. Anyway, we mixed a healthy dose of self-interest in the commitment recipe, right off the bat.

I can't remember doing much of anything for my children that wasn't embroidered with a selfish stitch. From the first day they got inside my range, they were expected to bring me my fair share of fatherly gladness. When I pushed them to do well, I wanted to enjoy being the father of children who did well for themselves. When, high-minded, I held up virtue as the gold medallion of the contest of life, I was hankering to be the father of moral virtuosos. "Do it for the old man!" When I applauded them, I celebrated my own pleasure in them. When I worried about them, I fretted at the pain of being worried as much I feared for their safety.

My ego flowed through my commitment to them the way the juice of the grape flows through wine. Nothing for which to apologize; it's the bifocal way we love. And it doesn't shave a sliver off our commitment.

Some parents expect their children to provide them with immortality. Be their life beyond the grave.

Take my mother-in-law. She was well known in her circles as a woman who lived for her children, thought only of them, did everything for them. Nobody could have been more committed to her children than she was. And she was a believer too, always sang gladly the songs of heaven's joys.

But when she, on several occasions, summoned her children to her bedside, it being dying time now and then, my mother-in-law took their sorrowing presence as the right time to tell them again about her secret expectations of life everlasting. On each tender occasion she confessed that what she wanted more than anything else was for them to be her extension beyond her seasons of sojourn on this earth. Thus she coiled the reward of immortality *for herself* inside her selfless commitment *to her children*.

Every parent keeps a self-serving dream in the shadows of his or her unconditional commitment. No shame in it. And if we know that our free will offerings to the kids are investments in our own blessing, we can keep a sense of humor should the blessing ever be shrouded in sorrows.

Parents' commitments to their children are unlike any other commitment we make. No free commitment we make to any other person, is so caring and so controlling as a parent's commitment to a child. No other commitment is so self-serving and so self-giving in one gulp.

PARENTS ARE COMMITTED TO THEIR CHILDREN'S SURVIVAL NEEDS

Committed love goes into overdrive when it comes to things children need. How many good nights' sleep have we surrendered? How many dinners out, how many new cars, how many luring investments, how many unworried hours—things we wanted badly, things we figured we had a right to—how many have we surrendered to what we thought were our children's needs?

But it is not always easy to tell the difference between a child's desires and a child's needs. What does every ordinary child need? Special children need special things: a handicapped child needs things to compensate for nature's oversight, a gifted child needs special things to exploit nature's blessing. But there are some things—call them survival needs—all children must have.

Survival needs are what every child requires to keep body and soul together: food, liquid, elimination, warmth, and medication. But the heart has survival needs too: the comfort of another's voice, a song, a snuggle, a holding, a cuddling, and, above all, a reassuringly dependable presence. We do not have to dwell on survival needs; we all know that any parent is committed to meeting them.

Some parents are not able to keep this minimal commitment. They are too poor. They don't have enough food to give their children. They don't have a house in which their children can live. So when we talk about personal commitments on this primal level, we are also talking politics and economics. Some parents need a lot of help. Commitment keeping in the family ultimately becomes a political issue.

But children need more than sheer survival. They need what it takes to get them started on their path of growth.

Growth is not an optional luxury. When we stop growing we stop living—at least we stop living as human beings with a life's call to become what God has put it in us to be. So growth needs are, after all, survival needs. And every parent takes on a commitment to get a child growing.

How much and how far? Nobody can say for sure. It depends on a child's potential, on the family money tree, on the needs of all the other kids in the family. We cannot be specific. Growth is a matter of degree; every child has his or her own limits.

PARENTS ARE COMMITTED TO THEIR CHILDREN'S DREAMING

Once, when Charlie told me that he was going to be a big league baseball player, I said "Son, it takes very special stuff to play big league ball, and only a very few of the very best players ever make it." I wish I had told him to get his mother and me box seats at Dodger Stadium the year he got to the world series. I tried to protect him from his dreams; of all people, I should have known better.

I grew up believing that a child's dreams are land mines of pride sown by the devil in our souls. To dream the impossible dream was a way of challenging God, hubris, not nice for God's humble children.

I remember the first day of school after the summer of 1937. I entered high school that year, and in the first hour of English composition, Mrs. Sheridan told us all to write a short story of our lives, then and there, in class—her way of finding out who she had on her hands that term. I wrote down the first things that blew into my head and, looking the other way, I handed my paper to Mrs. Sheridan as we shuffled past her.

The next day she read some of our stories out loud, without telling us who had written them. She read mine, second of the lot. Only she and I knew that the words she was reading were my words. Our secret. It has bonded her to me ever since. And I have seldom again felt the flush of unexpected blessing I felt that day as I listened to her heavenly voice reading aloud to other kids the words I had written on a piece of paper.

As we left the room, Mrs. Sheridan took me by my biceps, held me just long enough to break my stride, and said, "Lewis, you write well." Just that, no more, no prodding me to keep up the good work, just that astonishing pat on the back: you write well. And she let me go.

No one had ever told me that before. No one had told me that I did anything well. But Mrs. Sheridan had and she didn't even know me. She gave me my first dream.

I got high on her affirmation, lost all my fear of pride and, that night at supper, told my family about my new dream. As I said before, we were not a dreaming family, so when I let my dream out of the bag, and told everybody that I just might become a journalist, write words for a living, it strained the family devotion to humility.

"Oh, Lewis, you shouldn't get such big ideas into your head. Don't be proud. Don't dream big-shot dreams."

They were right, of course, I knew in my heart that they were right. Mrs. Sheridan didn't really know. It had been an accident. Journalism was way beyond me. Maybe something else, something humbler, would turn up.

No parent was ever more committed to any child than my mother was committed to me, but she couldn't defy humility. To encourage a boy to dream was to set him up for the demons of pride, and for disappointment to boot.

A child, it seems to me now, has a right to his dreams. They are his own; he needs no protection against his dreams, only against those who would, if they could, save him from them. Dreams are visions by which ordinary kids grow, the lure of the impossible that, when we reach for it, makes more things possible than we dared believe. Parents are committed to let their children dream their wonderful dreams.

PARENTS ARE COMMITTED TO THEIR CHILDREN'S MEMORIES

We know who we are only if we have a memory. A memory we can claim as only our own. Mull it over. Embroider it. See ourself in it. A memory that tells us how our story began and where we fit within it.

Parents are committed to giving their children memories because a child has to write his own story out of the raw material of family memories.

A family is really a story, and a child's memory is a limited edition of his family's story. Every new generation writes a new chapter. But to write their own chapter, children have to know the chapters that went before theirs. This is why we need to hear about the olden days. We need a beginning for our own stories.

The best stories I ever heard were the stories my mother told us about when she was a little girl in the village of Rottevalle in faraway Friesland. Stories about how she floated down a river in a chicken coop, washed into the current by heavy rains, caught in the coop with a hundred hysterical hens.

Not a glamorous story, but it told me something about her, and so it told me something about me. There were others too. Stories about the long ice skating races down the frozen Frisian canals. Stories about a grandmother who was actually operated on for cancer without anesthesia, because if she was going to go to God she wanted to be awake for the trip. I needed the family stories, I think, because they gave me a bigger story inside which to fit my little story.

Doris and I visited Friesland a while ago, with our two boys. One dark and blustery afternoon, we walked through a cemetery lined with tilted, pockmarked marble slabs, where a number of my mother's folk were buried, going back a century or two. Charlie hustled from slab to weather-ravaged slab to take pictures of the ones that had his grandmother's family name, Benedictus, faintly readable, chiseled on them. Doris and I watched and wondered why he wanted snapshots of tombstones stuck on graves of people whose blood did not flow through an eddy of his own veins.

I think now that he needed to gather material for his story, the family story that he was a character in and had to play his role in, no matter how he had gotten into the plot.

We all need our memories because we all have our stories to write. It is a great evil to deny a child his memories.

A parent can steal a child's memory. Abuse a child and you rob her of her most important memory. She can't begin writing her own story where every child has a right to begin. She has to censor the opening paragraphs. Nobody can write her story with gladness if she cannot begin at the beginning.

There is only one way to get back the beginning of her story. It is the cure called forgiveness. Children need to forgive their parents, if only to get their memories back. And then go on to write their own stories, with the future chapters connected to the past the sad way, but the real way, it was.

PARENTS ARE COMMITTED TO TELL THEIR CHILDREN WHAT IS WORTH DYING FOR

Children have a right to know what their parents believe is worth living for. And dying for. Parents are committed to telling them.

It's not as though parents always know what is worth dying for. Lord knows, we give our children a lot of wrongheaded notions. But if we do not tell our children what we believe matters most of all, we tell them that nothing in life matters much more than anything else.

We are talking about character here, for one thing, about being a good person, not looking good, not feeling good, but *being* good, which is something else again. Character is about being a person who can spot the difference between honesty and hype even when experts tell us a lie for a good cause. It is about being a person who can smell a seduction for what it is even when it comes as an offer nobody could refuse. It is about being a person who has a feel for when something is wrong even when it's legal. And above all, it is about being a person who knows what the real difference is between loving people and using people.

Where the nuts and bolts of right and wrong fall into place inside the complicated issues that bedevil modern times is really not all that important here; we will forever dispute about them.

What counts most is character, becoming a person with an in-grained sense for what is fair and what is helpful in the ways people treat each other.

Let us say that a child asks whether she is permitted to do this or that. The parent says "No." The child asks, "Why not?" The parent says, "Because it isn't right." That's all. Explanations can come later. So can the arguments. Repeat the theme in any of its boundless variations, and the child will get to know one thing for sure: her parents believe that being right is more important than being rich, and that doing right is all about being the sort of person other people can count on to keep some decency and fairness and kindness alive in a world where, when people are not good, life goes to the dogs.

That being settled, a child is free to go on to write her own story, but whatever her story turns out to be, it will have a thread of decency and fairness that will tie together the loose pieces of the plot.

We are also talking about faith, about our restless heart seeking its peace with a personal power of love beyond what anybody can manage on earth. Everybody believes in *something*. Our children have a right to know what we believe and every parent is committed to telling them.

Before we put fork to plate at any meal in my mother's house, we folded our hands, closed our eyes, bowed our heads, and mumbled, each of us in turn: "Heere, zegen deze spijs, Amen." Lord, bless this food, Amen. And she never allowed us to push our chairs back and bolt from the kitchen table until we bowed again and muttered, "Heere, wij danken U voor deze spijs, Amen." Lord, we thank you for this food, Amen.

It was our ritual, our immigrant litany. It mattered little that we did not know exactly what we were saying. We were being given the raw material for our story, we were learning who we were; and however our stories would end one day, they would have to come to terms with every meal time when we put our scrawny heads down to pray in words we could barely translate.

The last scene of every day at our house was my mother's lonely summons to heaven for mercies on her five children. She would get on her knees in front of a rickety kitchen chair, put her elbows on the seat, bend her neck back, tilt her face to the ceiling, and make her pitch to the Lord in the inchoate groanings of a bone-tired Frisian widow. I could hear her prayers and feel the pathos from where I slept, just off the kitchen. The only words I recognized for sure were "Heere Jezus" and the names of each of us five kids, in order of birth, me last. And I knew that deep in her heart she depended on the Lord, *de lieve Heer*, to take care of us. And of her. And of the whole wide world.

My mother believed that her life and ours were nestled in the unseen arms of the Lord, that every good thing in life came from him, that whatever we took from him needed his blessing if it was going to do us any real good, and that we should be ever thankful for whatever gifts his tender mercies assigned to us. What matters was that it was not only what she believed in her own private soul, but what her family believed before her, to the third and the fourth generation, the family in whose line we located our being. What mattered is that in those prayers we were learning who we were, where we came from, and where we were going.

Clearly, my point does not depend on whether my mother taught me the true faith. The point is that she taught me *her* faith and the faith of my people. She was handing down to me priceless data about who I was and where I came from and where I stood with her before the Lord of heaven and earth. She was giving me the spiritual stuff for the writing of my own story.

Whatever shape or form I gave to my story thereafter, the raveled twine of every chapter is still wound—one way or the other—around the words I slurred at her behest three times each day, "Heere, zegen deze spijs."

Her faith was the core of her story, so she was committed to give it to us. In her fashion, she kept the commitment well.

PARENTS ARE COMMITTED TO THEIR CHILDREN'S FREEDOM FROM THEIR COMMITMENT.

Here is the paradox of parental commitments. By making their commitment, parents control a child's life. But they are, by that same act, committed to free the child from their control.

Personal freedom is power. An inner power for writing one's own story. It is the power to write our own real story out of the raw material we were given without being asked.

We are all a little scared when we set our children free to write their own stories. For they may use their freedom to walk a road we never walked, nor wanted them to walk. Their story may not be at all like our stories, or stories we ever dreamed of writing for ourselves. But when they write it responsibly, and honestly, out of the raw material we gave them, we can be thankful that we have kept our commitment to them.

Some parents have to push a child into freedom. A kid sometimes wants the freedom of options, consumer's freedom, but doesn't dare take on the freedom of inner power, the responsible person's freedom. So in order to keep our commitment to our child, we may have to shove him or her into freedom, the way a mother bear, at the right moment, pushes her cubs away.

I watched a close friend suffer through this apparent contradiction in commitment. He felt stuck with an older child, and wanted him out of the house. But the son was afraid of freedom; the prospect of being responsible for himself immobilized him. But he did want consumer's freedom, the choice of things to own and enjoy. So he climbed the walls to get freedom of choice, and he burrowed himself inside the family to escape freedom *for* responsibility. Meanwhile, he hated his own dependence and hated his father for pushing him toward freedom.

Finally my friend told his son, "For both our sakes, you have to go. Where? We'll find a place. But by April 30 you have to be gone."

He told me later, "Never in my life have I been so scared, so uncertain, felt so guilty. But we did it. And it worked."

Pushing children away from our controlling commitment is not a failure of commitment; it is the final step in commitment keeping. We don't stop caring, Lord knows. But we start caring in a style that matches their readiness for freedom.

Let's stop here before we go on to the next chapter, and remind ourselves what this chapter has been about.

Its been about the kinds of commitments that parents make to their children.

The sort of commitments they make match the sort of calling parents have. Their commitments have an unconditional, controlling, self-interested character. And what they commit to is not all that complicated. Every parent, simply by accepting the job, commits himself or herself to provide the children certain basic things every child has a right to receive, as a matter of course: what he or she needs to survive, permission to dream, memories with which to begin his own story, a share in his parents' faith, and the freedom to write his own story.

Remember Fred Fergusen, the man who felt like a failure at fathering, even though his children did him proud? Well, Fred has a lot of company.

Take my own mother. A parental saint, in her way, if you canonize people for doing what they had to do under the limits of what they could do. Yet when she looked back on her own parenting she felt a sorriness about it all, and a need to tell us about it, as if she were begging our pardon for what she had made of us.

So I would ask her, "What was it that you failed at, Mother? Can you give me a 'for instance?' "

She would shake her head as if she were trying to shake my question, like water, out of her ears. "Oh Lewis," she would say, "don't ask me any questions, just let me tell you that I failed to be a good mother."

Now for her, back in the Depression days, commitment was mostly a matter of seeing to our survival. Come October, would she get coal in the cellar before winter? Would there be beans and bacon and now and then, on Sundays, a pot roast on the table? Would there be cash for the summer property taxes? There usually was, every year. She kept her commitment to our survival, hard as it was to pull off in those days.

And not only to our survival. She made no bones about what she believed was worth dying for and worth living for. She gave us some wonderful memories, raw material for our stories, and set us free to write them for ourselves. And we knew she would be there for us, dog tired, at the end of every day's scrubbing; we never wondered whether she was coming back. All right, she was afraid to let us dream our dreams, and I'm sorry about that. But she only wanted to guard us from the demons of a proud heart. Nobody wins at everything.

Why, then, did she feel like a failure? Why do people such as Fred Fergusen and myself, and too many other parents who kept their commitments, feel like failures at commitment? For two reasons, only two, and simple ones to understand. For one thing, we measure our commitments against a fuzzy, globbish, impossible touchstone of perfection. For another, we shun the special grace God has for imperfect parents committed to imperfect children in an imperfect world.

Part 3

THE CRISES OF COMMITMENTS

CHAPTER 10

When Two Commitments Collide

We get caught, sometimes, in a commitment squeeze. Two commitments claim us at the same time, when we can keep only one of them. Commitments bring conflict into our lives.

We can't get away from it.

For one thing, we are limited; our supply of energy is limited, our time is limited, and our understanding is limited. So we may be forced into a conflict between what we *should* do and what we *can* do. For another thing, we make commitments to more than one person. Different sorts of commitments, for different sorts of relationships. And sometimes we are caught in the middle of them.

In this chapter we will look at some typical conflicts committed people get into, and see how—or whether—they can be resolved.

CONFLICT OF CIRCUMSTANCES

We can get into conflict simply because we make too many commitments. We can be heedless, even compulsive, about commitments; we can make them without regard to our own limitations, and without asking ourselves whether we have the time and the ability to do justice to any one of them.

I have an acquaintance who is the most committed person I know—if you gauge commitment by numbers. He is usually a little muddleheaded about them, and as a result he lets people down. But he expects them to let him off the hook because, after all, he is so terribly committed. In fact, he intimidates people with his prodigious ability to make commitments. So they excuse him: "Oh, Manny, well, the man has so many commitments, we shouldn't expect him to show up here for us." So he gets away with not keeping commitments because he is such a committed person.

It is a ruse. He does not let people down because he is too committed; he lets people down because he is not responsible. He makes too many commitments to too many people.

But there are also times when two reasonable commitments made by a responsible person simply get in each other's way. We can't keep both of them, at least not the way both people expect us to keep them. Circumstances force the conflict.

Here is a doctor utterly committed to his daughter, and certainly committed to be at her wedding. But he is also committed to a patient who has a heart attack two hours before the wedding. He has to decide between keeping his commitment to his daughter and keeping another kind of commitment to his patient. Whatever he does will let one of them down. He doesn't give up his commitment to either of them; but he has to say no to what one of them expects from him at this moment.

The doctor is not overcommitted. He has made reasonable commitments, but he is paying the price for being a limited person trying to keep commitments in a world where things can happen at the wrong time. Whichever person he chooses to be with, he will have to trust the other to understand, and if she cannot understand, to forgive.

Commitment keepers need to be tough. We cannot meet everybody's needs all of the time. And if we try to meet them all, we probably will not meet any of them well.

I am committed to my students. But I sometimes have to say no to a lone student who needs my help at an hour when I need to get ready to deliver a lecture to a room full of other students. On the other hand, that individual student's need may be so urgent that I will give him or her all of my attention even if I have to stumble through my lecture.

My limits force me to choose between specific claims that people have on me at a moment when their claims conflict with each other. I did not create my limits. Nor did I create the conflict. So, while I may regret having to make the choice, I feel no guilt for the choice I make.

CONFLICT OF LOVE

Walter wept, with deep, guttural groans. His face was pinched by the pain of a love he could not have. He had fallen in love with a woman. But he was committed to another. And he wasn't bearing up well in the conflict.

Walter is a minister, and a good man, a man of sorrows for the sorrows of his people, too sensitive for easy survival in his line of work. He cannot immunize himself against other people's pains; when they are bruised by the slings of fortune, he feels their wounds. And because he is open to their pain he is also open to their love.

His wife, Sherry, unlike him, bangs through life with a head of steam heated by fires burning in the belly of a midlife mother making a last-ditch try at making a paying career for herself. So she has little time to give Walter the lingering tenderness a sensitive person needs.

He had not been aware of any hankering for last-chance love, but he was certainly ripe for it, and it came to him in the generous affections of Marian, a woman widowed early, and to whose untimely loss Walter ministered. He brought manly compassion to her womanly sorrow; she answered with the gift of a woman's affection. He aches for this loving woman. And he is willing to give up everything to be with her, everything except one, his commitment to Sherry.

Love can be a terror when it runs head-on against a promised love. Fyodor Dostoyevski, the incomparable Russian novelist, fell totally in love with a married woman, could not have her, and wrote of his pain to a friend. "In all my life, I have never suffered so much. . . . My heart is consumed by deathly despair. . . . Oh! Let God preserve everyone from this terrible, dreadful emotion. Great is the joy of love, but the sufferings are so frightful that it would be better never to be in love." Walter too wished to God he had never known such love.

When righteous people judge those unlucky enough to have fallen ill with illicit love, they see it as a vulgar lust.

But Walter's love felt to him as pure as it was passionate, and more true than any proper love he had known. He did not feel like a David lusting at the sight of a naked Bathsheba; more like the poet Dante longing for the pious Beatrice. Had it been mere lust, he would have stuffed his libido into the gulag of his conscience, and repented of it. His love was beautiful; but it ran afoul of commitment, and the conflict was Walter's sorrow.

If I had not believed in commitment, I might have told Walter something like this: "Walter, it's a choice between desires; you have to decide what it is that you really *want*. Do you want the security of a stable marriage, without much fire in it, along with your job in the church? Or do you want your one chance at love?

No conflict of commitment, just a choice between what you want more and what you want less.

But Walter knows he has a conflict. He has a conflict because he believes in commitment and he wants love.

He takes the only cure consistent with his commitment. He breaks with desiring love and sticks with promised love. Spiritual surgery, total severence, awesome pain for Walter, of course, maybe even more for the woman he loves.

There is no anesthesia in spiritual surgery.

Commitment does not inoculate people against the pain of competing loves. Commitment often has to surmount and survive the conflict. Meanwhile, let him—or her—scorn the scars who has never felt love's wounds.

CONFLICT OF FAITH

His name is Asher Lev. He has a gift, a great gift. But where does his gift come from?

Asher Lev is Chaim Potok's Hasidic Jewish prodigy from Brooklyn, the boy with a magnificent gift for painting what he feels and what he sees, the hero of the moving story *My Name Is Asher Lev*.

Hasidic Jews do not paint pictures. They study Torah, they live Torah, they live for the One whom no one can see, and whose face no one can paint. Asher Lev's father lives for the Invisible One, the Ribbono Shel Olom.

To Asher's father, drawing and painting are foolish games for a Jewish boy to play. Maybe Asher's gift comes from the place of evil.

Asher Lev, though, cannot resist his high gift. A fierce power inside of him drives him to paint everything that has shape and form. Two times he paints nude women, and his pictures are hung in public. This offends his father deeply; he does not look at his son's painting, nor accept his son's gift as a gift of God.

But there is something worse, much worse, almost immeasurably worse.

Asher Lev is driven to paint his own family. Especially his mother, who has suffered much because she loves a husband of the forbidding Torah and a son with a forbidden gift. Asher has a need to paint his mother's pain.

He goes to Europe, and there he is captivated, obsessed even, by paintings he sees of the Crucifixion. He has never seen suffering expressed with such power. There is nothing like it in the Jewish tradition, nothing that can serve as a mold for the anguish and torment that he feels in his mother. He must paint her suffering in the form of a cross.

The painting becomes a sensation.

Asher's father comes to an art show and sees Asher's work. It is an abomination to him. He cannot see it as a painting. He sees a son who has betrayed the Torah, betrayed his people, betrayed his family, betrayed his father, by painting a crucifixion.

The talent is from the place of evil; he knows it now.

When Asher's father leaves the gallery, he does not look at his son. He closes the door of a cab in Asher's face, but does not look at him. The people of the synagogue also turn their faces away from him. The leader of the synagogue tells him he should go away from his people; he is an offense.

Asher moves away, to Europe.

His father does not speak to him when he goes.

How can a father keep a commitment of love and care for a son who denies a father's deepest faith, his truest life?

It is hard for a father and mother to separate themselves from that in which they deeply believe. It is hard for them to see that a child could walk a different path of faith without walking away from them.

I am very close to a man, a Christian, who had a heavy heart because his son did not believe in Christ. He had worried a lot early on when his son had used some drugs and walked an unsteady line at the edge of dropout. But the worry was nothing like the hurt he felt when he learned that his son could not share his faith.

He felt that his son's loss of faith must have been his fault. If he had only been a better father, lived more consistently, more attractively, his son would have remained a Christian. He was rejecting himself as a father, and projecting his own self-rejection on to his son.

My friend's false guilt led him to feel rejected by his son and his pain tricked him into rejecting his son for rejecting him. The conflict was played out entirely within his overloaded conscience.

It was healed there as well. With good counsel, and the discovery that even a "failed" father could forgive himself, my friend came to see that what had hurt him was not simply his son's inability to share his faith. What had hurt most was his wounded pride, his sense of failing at being the perfect father.

Once he was free from his guilt, he let his care for his son transcend the conflicts of their faiths. He visited his son, who had taken a job on the West Coast and, for the first time, as two adults, they talked, one about his faith and the other about his inability to share it. And their doubts, yes, *their* doubts. The conflict was not undone, but it was set out more plainly for each to see and feel for what it was.

Before he left, my friend took his son's hand and said to him, "I want you to know that your mother and I will always be there for you."

The son said, "I know." That was all. No more.

For my friend, it was an illumination: a son could turn away from a father's faith and not turn away from a father. A father could mourn a son's lost faith and not mourn his son. Caring between persons can survive conflict between faiths.

It isn't as hard on commitments as it used to be when two committed people belong to different sects of the same faith. In the old days Catholic parents would turn their backs on a daughter who married a Protestant boy. And Protestant parents would disown a boy who married a Catholic girl. But we have discovered that a conflict of tradition is not the same as a conflict of faith.

I have two friends who live near Nairobi, in Kenya; one of them, Debra, is a white woman, seriously Protestant, European, and the other, Joseph, is a black man, conscientiously Catholic, African. How unlikely just a little while ago that two people such as they would make and keep a commitment of lasting love to each other. But they did and they do, though only as they let themselves unite in a mystical reality at the core of their conflict.

They had to fumble through dark ditches of shared ignorance; neither of them had realized how little they really knew about each other's culture and faith. They tried at first to be beautifully accommodating; for instance, they would get themselves up on Sunday for early mass and then drive across Nairobi to the Presbyterian service. But it was all too contrived.

The Protestant larder was bare for Joseph. The Catholic table was too plush for Debra. He wanted eucharistic drama; she needed biblical teaching. He was bored by Protestant sobreity; she was leery of Catholic pomp.

So on Sunday mornings, Debra and Joseph walked their divergent churchly paths: he off to meet Christ in the early morning mass and she to meet Christ in the sermon at the indulgent hour of eleven.

The Mass, or communion, became the hinge on which the conflict turned. Joseph had been taught that the Catholic Mass transmitted to him the life blood of divinity. Debra had been taught that the Catholic Mass was a cursed idolatry. Two people, an African black man, a European white woman, with cultural gaps ten miles wide between them, found that it was not their races or cultures, but this ritual, in which all people were meant to find their oneness, that separated them.

Concord came in measured spoonfuls of spiritual discovery. Not whole hog, but in jerky illuminations. It took a move to the fringes of Nairobi, where, settled in, both Debra and Joseph had to find new religious places for themselves. They found one together, a Catholic–Protestant mixture, carried on at the edges of the establishment by a few charismatic nuns and sympathetic priests. Debra experienced an exuberant faith that zigzagged through human lives without regard to race or creed. And she began to see the Mass in different shades too.

What does it really matter, she mused, what anybody *thinks* about the Eucharist, as long as Christ, somehow, in secret shapes that escape every partisan model, is there in it, waiting for her? Freed for flying by the charismatic spirit, she took a huge eucharistic leap over her Calvinist trepidations; she knelt one Sunday morning, trembled, opened her mouth, extended a dry tongue just beyond her teeth, and invited a priest to set a delicate wafer on the tip of it; she received and ate the body of Christ.

The gap was bridged. At the heart of the matter, she could now be where Joseph was. The sacrament that had always been the tangible reason why Catholics and Protestants could not be one body had become the uniting force in the lives of two committed people. Debra is still Protestant, faithful to the core, and Joseph is still Catholic. The stuff that separates them is still lodged in the cerebral cortex of their faith. But the alienating dogmas are overcome by their shared spiritual reality. Planted in the soil of their mystical unity, their different traditions now nourish both their lives, the way a magnificent Lodgepole Pine and a Giant Sequoia planted in the same spot share a single source of life from their fused roots.

All well and good, but when a man feels that his wife's faith is a betrayal of the life they once shared, we do have a conflict.

Delores was born again while jogging down a grassy road divider of a Chicago suburb listening, for laughs, to an evangelist on her Walkman radio. Arad was Westernized, modernized, but still a Muslim by inheritance from his Pakistan family. When Delores began to tell him about the joys of her new faith, however, he became a passionate believer in Allah.

So Delores became a closet evangelical. She got into her blue-and-white warmup suit and went jogging every Sunday morning around ten. Before her breath came heavy, she broke stride and slid incognito into the back pew of the Church of the Savior in time to catch the sermon. Then she jogged back home and ate Sunday brunch on the patio with Arad.

Her devout deception was uncovered, however, when a jogging neighbor, puffing right behind her one Sunday morning, watched her cut away from the pack and skip into the open door of the sanctuary. He kidded Arad about it while they were carpooling down the Kennedy Toll Road into Chicago's loop the next morning. It was not a good Monday for Arad.

He waited until the next Sunday when she got back from

jogging, to tell Delores that her cover had been blown, and that she had become a heavy offense to his family.

So, since she had been pulled out of the closet anyway, Delores figured she might as well show all her Christian cards. She was, and Arad might as well get used to the idea, beginning to feel a call to Christian ministry, and had enrolled herself for a course in New Testament literature at a seminary in North Chicago.

Arad said nothing.

Next morning at breakfast he told Delores that he wanted her to cancel her seminary plans and quit the Sunday morning charade.

Delores said nothing.

That night, in bed, Delores told Arad that she could not cancel her plans. She was committed.

Arad spoke no more about it.

Each of them adopted a strategy of unconditional surrender. One of them had to change. But neither of them could. So the faiths that set them in conflict with each other were pitted against the commitment they had to each other. A negotiated compromise seemed impossible.

Another kind of crisis came into their lives, however, and the caring side of their strained commitment began to temper their hostility. Delores found a lump on her breast, had it diagnosed, and was told to get prepared for a radical mastectomy.

Arad's anger was washed in fear. Fear for her—would she survive? Fear for himself—could he be attracted to a woman without a breast? In his fear, Arad's anger died and when his anger died, his care came alive again.

Delores also learned something about caring, that it has a permissive phase. She had believed that if she cared enough for Arad she should convert him. Now she understood that care for someone gives him permission not to be converted. To be what he is and to believe what he believes. It took Arad a while to trust Delores's permissive care. But once he trusted it, he felt secure enough to give the same permission to her.

Conflicts of faith are not easy to negotiate within commitment. But they become negotiable when both persons care enough to permit radical difference. As of now, Arad and Delores, with caring permissiveness, are gradually reducing their conflict. The nuances of the compromise are worked out day by day, crisis by crisis, but the foundation has been laid. Two people's commitment to each other can transcend conflict of faith if their care means letting each other believe as they must believe.

CONFLICT OF DREAMS

Willy Lohman is a salesman first and always, and he is committed to his dreams for his two sons.

Willy's dream? Make it big on the basis of being liked. "That's the wonder of this country," he would say, "that a man can end up with diamonds on the basis of being liked." And Willy taught his boys all about how to get people to like them. "The man who makes an appearance in the business world, the man who creates a personal interest, is the man who gets ahead."

Biff is his favorite, but he can't make the crazy dream come true for Biff.

"Pop, I'm a nothing! I'm nothing, Pop."

Willy won't believe it. He keeps dreaming, dreaming lies, and forcing them on Biff as if lying dreams could create his reality.

Biff says he is leaving home, leaving his father alone with his pipe dreams.

"May you rot in h___," Willy says.

Biff leaves. Willy kills himself.

At the funeral Biff mutters, "He had all the wrong dreams, all, all wrong."

Willy and his dreams are not strangers among American fathers, which helps explain why Arthur Miller's *Death of a Salesman* is an American classic.

A father can even have dreams that his son will be a saint, or a leader, and it could all be a pipe dream if he is committed to his dream more than to his child.

John Adams, second president of the United States, dreamed that his sons would be great men. One of them, John Quincy, made the dream come true. But the two others, Charles and Thomas, did not have the stuff to be great. And John Adams took it personally.

When Charles lay dying in New York, John Adams refused to leave Washington and go to see him. He compared Charles to Absalom, King David's rebel son, and Charles came off the worse of the two. The king's son at least had "some ambition" the former president wrote. "Mine is a mere rake. . . . *I denounce him.*"

Break your commitment to your own son because he cannot make your dreams come true? Parents do it when they cannot keep their dreams separate from their ego.

Conflict of dreams! It happens on a smaller scale too.

I dreamed early on that my daughter would be a pianist and that my first son would be a lawyer and the second a historian. And my commitments to them got confused with a commitment to my dreams for them. So I had to cut away my dreams *for* my children from my commitment *to* my children. None of them even tried to make my pipe dreams come true. Good thing too.

A dream is a nice thing to have, for the dreamer, a floating bubble sometimes, quickly burst, and sometimes the seed of possibilities for the future. But we can get committed to our dreams. And commitment to our dreams almost always gets into a conflict with our commitment to our children.

CONFLICT OF NEEDS

FRANCES: I'm leaving you, Arthur. The only way I can survive is to get away from you.

ARTHUR: How can you simply run away? What about the vows you made to me? Doesn't your commitment mean anything to you?

FRANCES: Yes, Arthur, I've kept that commitment for twenty-two years. Now I need to keep another commitment.

ARTHUR: What commitment? How could you have another commitment?

FRANCES: I need to keep a commitment to myself, Arthur, can you understand that? To myself.

ARTHUR: How about me, Frances, have you thought of what you owe me?

FRANCES: Yes, Arthur, I've thought a lot about what I owe you, but right now I owe myself even more.

A lot of people are acting out this script these days. And a lot more are fretting about it. It suits the temper of our culture: "I've got to take care of myself."

Frances says that she is committed to herself. But what does she have in mind? Is she committed to her needs? Or is she only committed to her desires? And does she really know the difference?

There comes a time in every committed relationship when one person has to give up what he wants so that the other person can get what she needs. But he should not give up what he needs so that the other person can get whatever she wants. A commitment is not a blank check drawn on our needs so that another person can satisfy his or her desires.

The trick is knowing the difference between our needs and our desires.

When we want something badly, we *feel* as if we truly need it. The more addicted we are to things we desire, the more they *feel* like needs. A smoker only wants a cigarette, but she *feels* as if she needs it. A compulsive spender only wants to buy something, but he *feels* as if he really needs it. We are all in the same boat, one way or the other; we have a hard time seeing the difference between what we need and what we want.

Knowing that there is a difference comes with maturity. Knowing it is also crucial to the success of committed relationships. But nobody knows the difference with scientific precision. And we all get confused when our own desires are involved.

Let's try a rough definition. *Needs are what we require for living an essentially human life. Desires are what we require for living a pleasurable life.*

Now let's shake our rough definition down to four categories of basic human needs—four things we all need in order to be a functioning human being.

1. Survival needs: what we need to keep body and spirit together.
2. Moral needs: what we need to keep a sense of our personal integrity.
3. Power needs: what we need to take responsibility for our own lives.

4. Spiritual needs: what we need to relate to God in gratitude and love.

As for desires, the field is wide open. We can want what is good for us. We can want what is bad for us. We might want what other people think anyone would be crazy for having. We might want what almost everybody else wants. Wanting things is a terrific energy; it makes for exciting relationships. But if we confuse our desires with needs, and if our desires get in the way of the other person's needs, we have a conflict on our hands.

Some people sacrifice what they really need to their partners' desires, and put up with the unfairness for years. Then they suddenly discover that it's time for keeping their commitment to their own selves, time to tend to their own needs.

Which is what happened to Frances. For many years she surrendered two basic needs to Arthur's compulsive desires. She needed self-respect. And she needed integrity in her life. She surrendered them both.

Arthur had a strong desire to live well beyond their means. He drove a luxury car when he could hardly afford a subcompact. He bought four hundred dollar suits when he could hardly afford a new shirt. He also had a compulsion to let Frances know that she was inferior to him, not as well educated, not as talented, not as smart, and generally not quite in his class.

Frances finally decided that it was time to make her move, to keep a commitment to herself. First she tried to persuade Arthur that she had a deep need to respect herself, and that she needed financial honesty in her life. She tried for five years, but he would not change or could not change.

Failing to persuade him, she separated from him, to find her self-respect and, in the bargain, to gain some integrity in her life.

Arthur appealed to her commitment, and brought God in to support his case. She countered by saying that God had awakened her, as a person aroused from a coma, to her commitment to herself, and to what she needed.

Frances saw her conflict this way: all the years of their relationship, Arthur had pushed his two desires up against two of her needs, and her needs had always given way. Now she re-

sisted. She had a survival need to respect herself; she bucked
this need up against his desire to feel superior. She had a moral
need to live with integrity; she bucked this need up against his
desire to look rich while they could not pay their bills. And she
determined to no longer surrender these needs to Arthur's desires.

Of course Arthur *felt* as if he really needed the things he
wanted—to look rich and to feel superior to Frances. Neurotic
feelings, yes, but real to him. He was certain that they had a
conflict because she pitted her desires against his needs.

It might have helped had both Frances and Arthur observed
four basic ground rules for settling conflicts between needs and
desires.

1. *Desires give way to needs.* If getting what I want prevents
   you from getting what you need, I give up what I want
   so that you can meet your needs.
2. *Needs do not give way to desires.* If getting what I need prevents you from getting what you want, I do not give in
   to your desires.
3. *Desires are negotiable.* If getting what I want prevents you
   from getting what you want, we negotiate; neither of us
   surrender, both of us compromise.
4. *Needs are negotiable.* If getting what I need prevents you
   from getting what you need, we negotiate as equals, from
   strength to strength; we compromise our less basic needs
   so that both of us can meet our more basic needs.

If they had both lived by these rules from the beginning,
Arthur would not have expected Frances to surrender her needs.
And early on Arthur would have seen his neurotic desires for
what they were. In any case, Frances now refused to surrender
her needs to Arthur's compulsive desires. Nothing could be negotiated unless Arthur gained a better insight into his own desires.

Frances was committed to Arthur. No doubt about that at all.
Her conflict had come when she had awakened to a commitment
she owed to herself. She had kept faith with Arthur for more
than twenty years. But Arthur had never given her permission
to be faithful to herself. So she ended the conflict by ending her
commitment to Arthur.

Who failed to keep the commitment? Did Frances fail her commitment because she walked out on Arthur? Or did Arthur fail his commitment because he refused to honor the most basic term of all personal commitments—the surrender of our desires when what we want prevents another person from getting what he or she needs?

Sometimes our conflict is between each other's real needs. Not between your needs and my desires, but between your needs and my needs. The concrete question, then, is this: which need is more basic?

Our need to survive is obviously most basic. We need to survive as bodies. But we need to survive as spirits too. If one of us threatens the other's survival, in body or spirit, we may not surrender. Nor may we negotiate. The other person's lesser needs come second to our need to survive.

We have no need that presses harder on the core of our beings than our need to be at peace with the still, small voice of our conscience. It is our need to be at home with our deepest selves, whole, one, in unity with the moral core we sometimes call our heart of hearts. To separate our actions from our hearts is to slice ourselves apart. What we do, how we live, how we treat ourselves and others, how we live our lives, they all have to harmonize with the urgings of our hearts.

We cannot let ourselves surrender this need to anyone else's desires. Our moral needs are not negotiable. If someone to whom we are committed maneuvers us into a surrender, our inner voice will say, "Never," and it urges us to listen.

We need to have power, too; for instance, we need the power to make choices that affect our lives. We cannot surrender our power to each other. But power can be negotiated. When your need to be strong gets in the way of my need to be strong, there is nothing for us to do but negotiate from one another's strengths.

We can compromise our desires without surrendering our needs. We can compromise on our lesser needs without surrendering our basic needs. There is no end to negotiation; we have to keep at it as long as we are keeping commitments to one another. No commitment ever deserves total surrender, not of the things we need in order to keep our personal lives intact. But everything else is open ended. We need to care enough to negotiate. And care enough, too, to keep asking ourselves what the difference is between what we really need and what we only want.

CONFLICT OF CONSCIENCE

We can make commitments that violate our own conscience. And we ought to break them. There is no virtue in commitment to vice.

Albert Speer, brilliant architect that he was, spent most of a lifetime building Hitler's wretched Reich. But he repented, and when the Reich was crumbling around him, he wondered how he could have given his lustrous talents to this titanic evil.

He knew the answer. He tells us in his memoirs, *Inside the Third Reich*, that he made a commitment to Hitler once, and never let himself look twice at that commitment. Never examined it. Never questioned it. Never let his conscience get into an argument with it. Blind commitment explained his great evil.

There is no moral magic that makes every commitment worth keeping. Commitments are not good to keep simply because we made them sincerely. We can commit ourselves to evil things. We can commit ourselves to good things. Only commitments made to good things are worth keeping.

Besides, things that were good when we first made our commitment can go sour on us. Nothing is incorruptible. Every commitment we make is open to criticism. And we sacrifice something of our mature humanity if we do not dare criticize our own commitments.

Faust committed himself to the devil, and went to the edge of hell, keeping his commitment.

Agatha Fregosy committed herself to Jim Jones and the People's Temple. She died with all the other committed people, drinking poisoned Kool-Aid in Jonestown when Jones said, "Drink."

Every human being has a commitment to his or her own conscience. No other commitment, to a person or to a cause, deserves equal status with commitment to conscience. And because even a commitment that began well can be twisted into evil, we need to keep the eye of our conscience trained on it, lest keeping our commitment ends with losing our soul.

This chapter can be summed up very quickly: we make our commitments as limited people with limited power. We are often torn, not between keeping or breaking a particular commitment on its own merits, but between two commitments. Keeping one of them may require us to break the other.

It is the price we pay for being limited and flawed folk trying to be commitment keepers in situations that sometimes ask for more than we can deliver. More, sometimes, than we *should* deliver. There is no simple device which resolves all our conflicts. There is no single rule that must always be obeyed. And there is no person on earth with wisdom enough to know how the rest of us should resolve our conflicts. But the critical question in all conflicts is the question of care: do we care enough for each other to negotiate our way through the conflicts of our commitments?

CHAPTER 11

When Someone Breaks
Our Trust

Saints may never let us down. But how often do we commit ourselves to saints? Most of us commit ourselves to ordinary people and, sooner or later, discover that ordinary people let us down. Even decent people hurt each other. Sometimes they hurt each other deeply, and unfairly too.

There are pains inside any committed relationship for which there is only one remedy: forgiveness.

There are also pains for which forgiveness is not the right remedy.

We need to know the difference.

THE SORTS OF THINGS THAT NEED TO BE FORGIVEN

To put up with some things, all we need is a little generosity. A sense of humor. Some tolerance. Call it by its classic name: *magnanimity*. It means, literally, "a largeness of spirit." A magnanimous person is broadminded enough, generous enough, to live with failings in people. Quirks and cranks in persons we are committed to annoy us, but they don't kill commitment if we keep a modest measure of generosity in our styles.

Let's say that your husband has a compulsion to tell wornout, boring, maybe crude, stories that embarrass you when he tells them in the presence of your friends. Or that you are a tidiness buff, and your wife doesn't notice that the house is a mess when you are bringing home a guest for dinner. Or that your friend never shows up on time. These are fender benders in the cross-town traffic of a committed relationship, annoying things, but not capital offenses.

They are the unwanted annoyances that we can swallow with a spoonful of magnanimity, a little big-mindedness. But we mustn't confuse it with forgiveness. Forgiveness is a more serious mercy. Not for annoyances, but for the deeper wrongs that people do us.

We also need a simple grace to accept bad things for which nobody is responsible. Things we didn't expect, don't want, but things people cannot help. We don't forgive people for them, we accept them and adjust to them. They are the shadow side of any committed relationship.

If a woman's husband becomes impotent because he has prostate cancer, she may feel cheated, and she may have a problem she devoutly wishes would go away. But she accepts it as a severe handicap and makes the best of it. It is not a problem she can solve by forgiving him. If a man gets married with the dream of having five kids, and he discovers his wife cannot bear a child, he may feel stung by life's unfairness. But he accepts it as a deep disappointment and works around it. One thing he does not do is forgive his wife for what she cannot help.

Making accommodations to nature, living with mystery in the will of God, is sometimes what commitment keeping needs in a world that never quite measures up to our expectations. It asks a lot of us sometimes, and it certainly can seem unfair, especially when miracles don't happen for us. But sometimes making accommodations is the only way to play the game of life in commitment.

Sometimes people keep commitments in the painful spells simply by waiting them out. Waiting is love's less lyrical art. But, now and then, it's the only song we can sing. It is a way of caring when there is nothing else you can do.

Doris could tell you something about waiting. She waited about two years for me to get healed of a depression that made living with me heavy.

My depression was the exposed surface side of my smothered anger. Healthy anger is an energy that moves healthy people to change whatever it is that makes them angry. But I turned my anger inward, did nothing to change what hurt me, and got too depressed to change anything at all.

I was angry at a lot of things, all of them lumped into a self-pitying sense that I was a victim, bowed down by large lumps of life's crazy unfairness. Anger took control of my life, and shoved me, brooding, into a black hole of the soul where I surrendered to my sadness.

If I did not have the energy to lift myself out of the hole, Doris did not have the savvy to seduce me out of it. To shift metaphors, the river was mine to cross. So she just waited for me to wade or swim or float over it.

Love suffers long. How long? Long. But how long? Just long. Forever? Maybe not forever, but longer than we would wish. Longer than we could wait if we did not care enough.

Waiting paid off. I had good friends who helped me take some responsibility for myself. I experienced three weeks of intensive therapy that set me in the healing stream of self-forgiveness and self-acceptance. And I came back on my way to wholeness.

Doris kept her commitment *to me* by waiting *for me*. Just waiting. She did not wait because she felt pinned into place by a promise she had once made to me. She waited because she cared enough to wait.

In short, the only way to keep commitments to people, sometimes, is by indulging their failings, accommodating to their limits, and waiting out their neuroses. Because caring is the business of commitment.

But there are other times when only forgiving can do the trick. These are the times when someone hurts us deeply with a pain that we did not have coming, someone is responsible for the sting we feel. Forgiving is a gracious way to cope with deep pain that is unfair and for which someone else is to blame.

The toughest pain to heal in a committed relationship is the pain of betrayal—the wound of a broken trust.

When trust is broken, we choke on our own commitment. Betrayal builds a wall between us, around which we cannot maneuver. It digs an arroyo between us that we cannot bridge. It prevents us from keeping our commitment, because it separates us from the person who hurt us. And in our hearts we know why.

It is because our very selves are invested in a personal commitment. This illustrates the difference between a commitment and a contract: in a commitment we deal with our selves, in a contract we deal with goods and services. Betraying a commitment is infinitely different from not living up to a contract. If someone breaks a contract, we can go to court to get compensation. But who can compensate for broken trust?

When a friend tells our secrets to someone who could hurt us with them, she betrays us. When someone we trust brutalizes us, with his words or with his hands, he betrays us. When a partner demeans us and makes us feel less than any human being should feel, she betrays us. When a child we trust steals from us, lies to us, becomes our enemy, he betrays us. These are the offenses that break our trust and threaten our commitment.

The deep pain of broken trust has one cure, only one. It is the remedy we call forgiveness.

Forgiving is love's way to heal ourselves of pain we did not deserve, cannot overlook, and cannot forget, a pain for which we hold someone responsible, a pain for which we blame someone.

IF WE FORGIVE, SHOULD WE GO BACK?

The first person to benefit from forgiving is always the person who forgives. We purge our heart of the poison someone meanly put there. We lift ourselves from the bilge of hate and dance to the melody of inner healing. We set a prisoner free and discover that the prisoner was us. We create a new beginning for ourselves by unlocking the shackles that otherwise would hold us tight inside a painful past. Forgiving is for the offended, first. Later, for the offender.

Let us suppose, then, that we have forgiven someone to whom we were committed. The critical question is, should we renew our commitment to someone who betrayed our trust? Or is it better, sometimes, to forgive and say good-bye?

Take adultery, for example. Can commitment survive adultery?

Adultery slices so fiercely into the tender tissues of trust that we can go on with our commitment only after our injured spirit agrees to the soul surgery we call forgiveness.

But even if we can forgive, we need not always be reconciled. It may be better, sometimes, to forgive and, having healed ourselves, take our leave.

It all depends.

For one thing, married people make wayward love for many reasons, and with many motives. So we need to know what he or she was up to.

Take Chad, for instance; he was married to an utterly committed woman named Ginger for five years and for three of the five he maneuvered himself into three separate love affairs on the side.

What is more, he made very little effort to hide his philandering. Why would he leave letters lying open in his dresser drawer? Why would he charge local motel bills to his MasterCard? Did he want Ginger to know?

Making love to other women had nothing to do with loving them, and everything to do with hurting Ginger. He never missed a chance to tell her that she was overweight, stupid, and a lousy housekeeper, not at all what he had wanted in a wife, and certainly not what he deserved. Naturally, he hinted, with all the subtlety of a sledgehammer, anyone stuck with an unsatisfactory woman had the right to look for a little satisfaction outside the bonds.

Chad killed both components of personal commitment: he was inconsistent and he did not care.

What Chad told Ginger was basically what she had heard from her own parents anyway. She "knew" early on that she was an unsatisfactory person. She swallowed whole the depressing proposition that she deserved the misery Chad made her feel.

Finally, though, she went to a counselor recommended by a woman she had met at her hairdresser's. And she harvested enough insight from him to see the truth. The turning point of her illumination was this: Chad was the culprit of the piece, not she, and she should not let him get away with it anymore.

But suppose that Ginger had slowly found the grace to slowly forgive Chad. Would the fact that she forgave him give her reason to renew the lease on her commitment to him?

If forgiving obligated Ginger to go back to Chad, then forgiving would not be a good idea. But forgiving does not turn forgivers into doormats; if it did, we would be better off leaving it to priests. Forgivers are not fools who suffer gladly. They may forgive but they do not go back to ask for more.

Chad killed Ginger's commitment; it is dead. Covenants can be broken so badly in human relationships that they cannot be revived. Not even forgiveness can bring them back to life. And forgiving doesn't obligate us to try.

Let's compare Ginger's situation to someone else's, Harry's, for example. Harry's wife, Janice, made love to another man. But Janice was committed to Harry, and to their marriage.

Recently Janice had been hired as a writer for an advertising agency in Des Moines, Iowa, where she and Harry live; Harry himself had urged her to try her writing wings there. After all, she had written a column for the *Cole College Chimes*, and being a lively campus reporter was the first thing about her that had caught Harry's fancy. Then Luke Simmons, over at the agency that ran ads for Harry's Honda dealership, mentioned that he was looking for a commercial writer—Janice's chance.

Her boss recognized real, if raw, talent when he saw it, and financed a weekend for Janice at a writers workshop in Los Angeles.

There she was, alone, where nobody knew her, when at the very first session she met one of the workshop speakers, a professional writer, with wily charms the like of which she had never had to cope with in Des Moines, a man who actually wrote for films in Hollywood, the big time. She saw him again at poolside, accepted his invitation for a little tennis before dinner, after which she sipped a little Chablis with him, which she wasn't used to because she and Harry had never gotten into wine at home. Anyway, before she realized what was happening, she felt a fever rising such as she had now and then fantasized, but with which Harry had never infected her. Ere the workshop had run its course, Janice found herself in bed with a genuine Hollywood screenwriter.

Saint Paul once said that people are sometimes "overtaken in a fault," which hints that good people may now and then act out of character; what they do is inconsistent with a commitment, but does not destroy it. Janice fell into a fault because she did not look where she was going. But she is not an honest-to-goodness adulteress any more than a woman who fixes a dripping faucet is a plumber. She was inconsistent, but she still cared.

When the Sunday morning sun rose high over the California coast, she recalled how, back home, she and Harry would at that very moment be on their way, hand in hand, to the second service at First Baptist, and she was trodden by the Four Horsemen of Guilt.

She told her workshop lover to go away and not come back, and vowed then and there to tell Harry what had happened and beg him to forgive her even though she knew she was less worthy of mercy than the chief of sinners.

She changed her reservation, packed, and left that morning, before the last plenary session, during which examples of the best workshop writing would be read aloud; she left even though she knew that one of her pieces had been chosen to be read.

Once she got home and was settled in, and after Harry had watched "Sixty Minutes," Janice told him, trembling as she went, just what had happened. Harry couldn't believe it was real, but, finally bowing to the truth, he bolted for the bathroom, where he vomited. Then he got in the Accord and drove around Des Moines for an hour, stopped for a cup of coffee, couldn't think of anywhere else to go, drove home, and went to bed alone on the davenport in the study.

Next day Harry went back to the Honda dealership, Janice went back to the ad agency. She waited alone in her private emotional wasteland to see what Harry would do.

After three weeks of Harry's stiff-upper-lip silence, Janice broke down and begged him to take her back into his life. Actually, Harry had been crawling a yard or two a day down the mercy road of forgiveness anyway. So when Janice begged, he told her he had already forgiven her, confessing that he himself had lusted now and then when he took an attractive woman for a test drive in one of his Hondas.

That night Harry and Janice made love with a zeal such as they had not known in the days of Janice's innocence. And they began their love again a few steps farther along on the path of kept commitment.

Forgiveness, for Harry, was a return-trip ticket back to the commitment he and Janice had made to each other.

Now let's go back a moment to Chad and Ginger. Why didn't

the miracle of pardon bring them back together? Why didn't it do for them what it did for Harry and Janice?

A few years ago in my book *Forgive & Forget: Healing the Hurts We Don't Deserve*, I said something about what it takes to be reconciled after we forgive. The words still sound right to me.

When you forgive

> You hold out your hand
> to someone who did you wrong,
> and you say: "Come on back,
> I want to be your friend again."
> But when they take your hand
> and cross over the invisible wall
> that their wrong and your pain
> built between you,
> they need to carry something with them
> as the price of their ticket
> to your second journey together. . . .
> What must they bring?
> They must bring truthfulness.
> Without truthfulness, your reunion is humbug,
> your coming together is false.

Janice brought truthfulness. Chad brought a lie.

The forgiving we do to heal the wounds in our memory has no strings attached. But reconciliation does: it needs truthfulness as the *fulfillment* of our forgiving.

FORGIVING OUR CHILDREN

Let's put the forgiveness factor in a different setting now, and see what happens when a parent keeps a commitment by forgiving a child.

In a literal sense a committed parent cannot stop being a parent. A father cannot unfather himself. A mother cannot unmother herself. Parent and child are forever parent and child.

And yet sometimes parents need to perform the healing act of forgiving in order to keep their commitment to be a blessing to their children.

For a parent trusts a child as much as a wife trusts a husband, and trust can be broken in any family. When a child betrays a parent's trust, it calls for the same remedy as when husband betrays a wife. If a father cannot forgive a son, he cuts his child off from the blessing of his commitment.

Let's watch a final scene of Sophocles' tragic drama of King Oedipus, and see Oedipus disown his son, Polyneices. Polyneices had turned against his blinded father and driven him into exile from Thebes, where he had once reigned as king. Now the son, himself in exile, is on his knees begging his father to forgive and bless him:

> Compassion limits even the power of God;
> So may there be a limit for you, Father!
> For all that has gone wrong may still be
> healed. . . .
>
> Why are you silent? Speak to me Father!
> Don't turn away from me!
> For your own soul's sake, we all implore
> And beg you to give up your heavy wrath.

But the pain of betrayal is too deep, its unfairness too galling, and Oedipus's hate too violent. He can empty himself of bitterness no more than the ocean can empty itself of salt. Oedipus spits his last words:

> Justice still has a place in the laws of God.
> Now go! For I abominate and disown you!

Condemned by his father's curse, Polyneices goes. He dies. Oedipus dies too, unreconciled to his son.

Another king comes to mind, another son, too, and another betrayal, but another ending to the story. King David of Israel, like Oedipus, is betrayed by his son. Absalom, like Polyneices, drives his father from his royal city. And David, like Oedipus, is sent running from his own child.

David sends his army against Absalom. But David cannot curse his son. We hear him say, in the Second Book of Samuel: "Deal gently for my sake with the young man Absalom."

The general knows only military requirements, nothing of fatherly pity, and he runs Absalom through. David hears the horrible news: "And the king was deeply moved, and went up to the chamber over the gate, and wept; and as he went, he said, 'O my son Absalom, my son, my son Absalom! Would I had died instead of you, O Absalom, my son, my son!' "

A blessing in absentia! Posthumous forgiveness. David could not dam the flow of his committed love.

The difference between Oedipus and David is, at heart, a difference of faith. Oedipus believed in fate. David believed in God. Fate does not forgive, so Oedipus cursed his son. A heavenly Father forgives, so David forgave.

There is still another story of a father's committed love, and it shows how forgiving and waiting can get nicely blended in the dynamics of a father's wounded love.

It is the story of the prodigal son, the empty-headed ingrate who cashed in what he had coming of his father's estate, and then went off to waste it on wild living.

The prodigal son was a fool, but not a traitor. He slinked away alone; he did not run his father off his own land. He was not in Absalom's class.

Still, he poured contempt on his father's commitment, and went off to a far country as a son who never had a father.

When the prodigal ran out of cash, saw what a mess his life had come to, he swallowed the dried pods of his pride, covered his bets, and crawled home. What could he lose?

His father saw him coming in the lengthening shadows of the olive trees, a bent stick slouching homeward. And he went out to meet his son, loping, his robe pulled up over his knees, arms akimbo, and looking like no Hebrew patriarch with a smidgen of dignity should ever have looked. He swallowed his wasted son in his arms before his son got to the estate gate, kissed his road-smudged mouth, and brought him home. And in the Gospel of Luke we hear him say to the servants of the clan: "Bring quickly the best robe and put it on him; and put a ring on his hand, and shoes on his feet; and bring the fatted calf and kill it, and let us eat and make merry; for this my son was dead, and is alive again; he was lost and is found.

The father blessed his wastrel son. But did he forgive him the way a man forgives an enemy? Or did he celebrate the ending of a long time of worried waiting? Something like forgiveness was happening. In the father's heart it must have felt like the healing of a hurt he hadn't deserved to feel. More like the joy of tender mercy than the relief of a waiting that was over.

I watched a father cope with a similar pain. He loved his seventeen-year-old son, Gerry, more than he loved his own life.

But Gerry wasted himself in the far country of his mind, not on wine, but on drugs, not with loose women, but with harmful friends.

He didn't betray his father the way Absalom betrayed David, and didn't squander his inheritance the way the prodigal son did, but was the pain any the less for it?

And what of the lies that every kid on drugs tells his—or her—parents? And what of the times he sneaked into his parents' bedroom and snitched cash from their dresser drawers? Is this the stuff of which betrayal is made? Or is it only the desperation of a young person backed against the wall of an expensive delinquency?

What did these fine points of morality matter to a wounded father?

So he waited. Stuck with terror in his guts, he waited. Against his powerful desire to wring Gerry's neck, against every self-defensive impulse to send him packing, he waited. He was never sure how long he should wait. But he stuck with what he was stuck with. And when Gerry came to his rightful mind, his father blessed him.

In the muddle and rumpus of family life, the nice distinctions between forgiving and waiting sometimes get fudged. No matter. A parent's commitments are seldom kept for long without a little forgiveness, now and then with massive doses. And sometimes we keep the commitments by just waiting out the bad times.

FORGIVING OUR FRIENDS

Forgiving can be hazardous to friendship. Forgive friends too quickly, too often, and you become a nag. And no one wants a nag for a friend.

Friendship survives on a diet of accommodation, of being generous about faults. Magnanimity again; show me a person big-minded enough not to require good friends to be perfect people and I will show you a friend who can keep a commitment to friendship.

There is such a thing as expecting too much from friends.

Not every friend has a perfect sense of timing; some friends tend to be late when we very much want them to be early. Not every friend remembers to return things she borrowed; some friends need nudging. Not every friend knows how to dress for the occasion; some friends are slobs. Not every friend invites you back after you entertained his out-of-town parents at a dinner party; some friends hate to entertain. Not every friend is a good listener; some friends talk too much.

We shouldn't forgive friends for being less perfect than we want them to be.

Nor should we forgive them for being more successful than we are.

Your kids dropped out of community college after the first semester; theirs are on fine scholarships at top-flight universities. And they never stop telling you how well their children are doing. You sweat blood just to pass every course; your best friend gets A's in everything without trying. And he pesters you for being too serious about your studies. Your husband is stuck at level C in a going-nowhere firm; your friend's husband gets periodic promotions and regular raises in salary. And she loves to tell you about their expensive vacations. You yearn for a little romance; your best friend is forever complaining about having too many men in her life.

It's hard to stay best friends with people who *always* do better than we do. But serious forgivers do not forgive friends for doing too well.

The sorts of things we need to forgive friends for are the sorts of things we would stop being their friends for—if we couldn't forgive them. It can happen when a friend betrays a trust.

The only way to rescue friendship from betrayal is by forgiving the betrayer.

But even when we do forgive him, we may be better off to call off the friendship.

Donald Dormer is a lawyer, a good one, but at this particular time he is wrestling with the kind of dilemma that takes more than a lawyer's skill to solve. Back in the early sixties he had gotten involved for a while with a radical protest group. He was a college student then, fed up with the system, and he had hooked up for a while with this group of bitter-end extremists. He didn't know what he was getting into at the time; and when he learned that this crowd treated people worse than did the system he wanted to change, he got out.

Then he applied for a job in the Justice Department, a job he wanted badly and one for which he knew he was qualified. But it called for security clearance.

He agonized over the situation, wondering if he should tell them about his brief romance with a radical organization. If he told he probably would not get the job. He wanted to be honest; but he wanted the job even more.

He talked it over with a good friend, a trusted friend. Her name was Judy, and she worked in the very department to which he was applying.

Judy advised him not to say a word. "That was in your previous existence," Judy assured him, "and nobody has to know about it. Why scuttle your chances?"

Donald went along, said nothing, got the job.

One fact Donald did not know was that Judy worked for a fanatic who expected everybody working under him to demonstrate his or her loyalty by exposing, once a year, at least one weak link in the security system.

Another fact Donald did not know about was Judy's problems with the boss. She had been feeling his paranoid breath, and she knew that what she needed right then was a chance to clobber a security risk.

Three months into Donald's new career, he got a letter telling him that he was fired. The reason: failure to disclose his 1962 membership in a radical organization.

Judy! Judy—Judas—he wanted to kill her and let her bowels gush over the steps of the Justice building.

Friendship is killed by betrayal.

Eventually, Donald may forgive Judy, begin the journey to his own recovery, heal his heart by purging his hate. Even wish Judy well. Someday.

But would his forgiving resurrect their friendship?

The odds are against it. And it would be right if Donald forgave from a distance, and buried the friendship. Not necessary. But right. Friendship can survive only so much.

But most friendships are tested by less grievous letdowns. We are not always sure of how to measure the disappointment, or how much to tolerate in a friend.

Some people lean too hard on friends, and expect too much from a relationship created to be equal.

They expect their friends to always pick up the tab, fix their plumbing and never send a bill, or drive them to work every day and never ask for gas money. And when their friends finally say no, they feel let down, badly treated, and wonder why their friends are not more committed to them.

One way to look at it is this: these are not the sorts of offenses that call for forgiving. They are annoyances that need understanding, indulgence too maybe, but not forgiving. Forgiveness is better kept for more serious stuff. Just understand that some people do not grow up, and that we are better off staying clear of them and choosing our friends wisely.

I will put this chapter in a nutshell. We keep our commitments in a world where even a decent person can let us down and betray our trust. When a person does, forgiveness is the way to cleanse our own heart. But forgiving someone does not necessarily mean that we should renew our commitment to him or her. For parents, yes; we should always try to bring a child back. But forgivers don't have to be friends again or spouses again, not when trust is shattered and there is no reasonable expectation of putting a shattered relationship together again.

We need a sense of humor to cope with those who annoy us, the patience to wait for sick people to be healed, and the grace to forgive those who betray the trust of our commitment. We also need the grace to renew our commitments when we can, and the wisdom to know when we should walk away.

CHAPTER 12

When What We Need
Most Is Hope

Every commitment we make is an act of hope. We make commitments because we hope that we can keep them. We keep them as long as we have hope that keeping them will bring good to both the persons we are committed to and to ourselves.

Hope is to commitment what gasoline is to the piston engine, and we can run out of both too soon. We can turn our solvable problems into incurable catastrophes before their time.

My son Charlie was a born problem catastrophizer.

We were all in our baby blue station wagon on the way to visit my mother in Muskegon one Sunday, the kids grumping in the rear, when Charlie bumped his head on John's elbow, broke his glasses, and cut his cheek. The blood dripped red on his clean shirt. Charlie saw the crimson tide and knew with intuitive clarity that he was a goner.

"I'm dying!" he yelled, "I'm dying!" Silence. Time for a serious reevaluation of the situation. And then, a wail from one who had slid into the other world: *"I'm already dead!"*

Premature capitulation to catastrophe.

Every counselor I know tells me that people struggling with their commitments tend too soon to see their problems as catastrophes and their commitments as dead or dying. They give up hope before its time.

In fact, the deepest reason behind what some critics see as our culture's copout from commitment is a loss of hope. Sociologist Christopher Lasch sees the symptom all around us, and speaks of it in his *Haven in a Heartless World:* "The ideology of [the uncommitted life] . . . radiates pessimism: the world view of the resigned." It makes sense. If we have given up hope for the future, why should we make serious, long-term commitments?

The critical question, then, is whether the future we can look forward to makes serious commitment a reasonable choice.

Let's admit that there are more than enough reasons to be pessimistic, for being afraid to make long-term commitments, for not wanting to take the risk. So before we talk about hope for *keeping* commitments, we should talk about fear, and about why people find *making* commitments a scary proposition.

WHY PEOPLE FEAR COMMITMENTS

People are edgy about commitments for a lot of reasons.

Some people have given up hope for the globe. They doubt that there is a future for life on earth. This is especially true of young people, and the more sensitive and aware they are, the harder it might be for them to keep hope alive.

Listen to Sam. "I would really like to make a permanent commitment to somebody, and live the kind of life with her that my parents have lived together. But my world isn't their world. They believe in the future. I don't. I think that some idiot in Washington or Moscow or some other place is going to push the button before too long. And there we go, the whole shooting match. So what's the point of making a permanent commitment to anyone?"

Sam isn't alone. If some polls are right, 75 percent of people under thirty expect the world to be destroyed before they can die a natural death. And they think that even if nobody is crazy enough to start a nuclear war, we will find other ways to make the earth uninhabitable. We will make the air unfit to breathe, the water unfit to drink, the food unfit to eat, and in general turn the globe into a glob of cosmic garbage.

With pessimism like this, commitment is going to need a powerful injection of hope if it is going to make a comeback.

But fear of commitment is also very private.

Some of us fear being abandoned.

Listen to Sarah. "I needed my father terribly, and he went out one night and took his life. He couldn't help it, I suppose, but he left me alone with nothing to hang on to, and I felt as if it were my fault that he did it. I'm not going to risk being left alone that way again."

Or to Frank. "My mother and father got into such awful fights, I was sure they were going to kill each other, and then my mother finally left and never came back again. It felt as if we kids didn't count at all, we felt like trash that could be thrown out with the garbage. So much for my parents' commitment. I am never going to put myself in that situation; I can't risk it. No commitment for me, thanks."

Fear of being abandoned! Reason enough to be skittish about long-term commitments.

And it's a reason more and more of us know personally. Polls show that 60 percent of the children born this year will spend at least part of their growing up with a single parent. Most of them will feel abandoned by somebody. By 1990, we are told, 70 percent of us will be part of a broken home—either our parents' or our own.

We are creating a cycle of commitment failure: the more commitments fail, the less courage we have to make them.

Some people are afraid to make commitments because they cannot trust *themselves.*

Listen to Linda: "I never stuck with anything. How could I stick with another person for the rest of my life?" Or to Steve: "The minute somebody starts getting thick with me, I have an urge to split. Whenever people start expecting me to be close, I begin to panic. Maybe commitments are just not my thing."

Fear of ourselves! How do we know we have what it takes to keep a commitment?

The answer is, we don't. Not for sure.

The question is, do we have enough hope to make the commitment anyway?

Commitments are a chancy thing in the best of times. But right now, in our kind of world, the only hope is hope itself.

Let's explore the ins and outs of hope, then, as the deepest secret of commitment making in a scary time.

The answer for many of us grows out of the soil of our faith. Do we believe that God is committed to us? Is he committed to keeping our world a place where making commitments to each other works? If God is really committed to us, and to our important personal relationships, we have reason for hope, and a reason for making commitments to them. So in my own experience, because I do believe in God, I have to ask whether my faith really does give me hope that keeping commitments is still the only way to keep our deepest human relationships alive and creative. I will talk about this more at the end of the chapter. For now, let's just explore what human hoping does for human commitments.

HOPE HAS TO BE REALISTIC

We are talking about hope that things can be better, not that things can be perfect.

Hope is not, in Voltaire's barbed words, "a mania for declaring all is well when things are going badly."

Once when I had about given up hope of ever understanding my adolescent tempest, Cathy, I asked my psychologist friend Paul Clement how a mixed-up father could get some insight into the turbulent mind of a teenager he loved. Clement, after all, was a professional, and I figured he ought to know. He said that there were three critical facts I had to remember about fathering rambunctious rebels. If I forgot any one of these, I would only add to my troubles. Here they are:

1. She is not human.
2. Survival is the best you can hope for.
3. Things are going to change.

Not what I expected from my friendly psychologist, and as I repeat them now, his words sound maybe too cute, maybe a little cruel. But they felt helpful to me then, because they made me feel that I was not alone among fathers in my frustrations, and that if this was the way things were, maybe I could cope. And when I came to put my own interpretation on his words, they made profound sense to me. For he was not describing my teenager; he was describing me, and my own unrealistic expectations.

Take the statement about teenagers not being human. It sounds, offhand, like a putdown. But it really had to do with me, and my crazy notions of what my daughter should have been. I expected her to be the rational, mature, sensitive human being that I thought every human being ought to be. But she could not be human in that way. Not then. Not yet. She could be, and was, a passionate person with a wild wave of anger at the unfairness of life, but she was not the reasonable human being I was unrealistic enough to expect her to be at that stage of her life.

Take the second point, too, about survival being all I should hope for. I came to understand it this way: I was having pipe dreams about enjoying a star for a daughter, well, not a star necessarily but at least a small asteroid up there in the select company of do-gooders, smiling at me while she grabbed her share of the prizes. OK, anybody can dream, but it was silly of me to ask for my version of the moon when I needed all my power just to stay on earth and be a friend to her on her terms.

Then the third part, that things would change. Well they did change, a lot, for the better. In fact, it's hard to believe now that I was dumb enough then to wonder if things were ever going to get any better. Paul Clement didn't promise me that *everything* would get to be just the way I dreamed it would be, or even that everything would change. He only said that *some things* would change. Which things? I'd have to wait and see. I did wait and I did see. And what I saw was enough to confirm my hope.

Anyway, that was how I kept my hopes within the limits of reality.

Hope is not a guarantee of complete satisfaction. It is a kind of power, an inner power to believe that life can get better, not perfect, just better than it is—good enough to make it worth the struggle to keep our commitment to someone about whom we care.

In fact, we are better equipped to keep our commitments if we come to terms with the likelihood that *some* things don't change.

Let's think a moment about things that don't change.

You used to be twenty-five, now you're forty-five; you can't go back, no use hoping. You've had a mastectomy and lost a breast; you can't get it back. Your husband has incurable erotic burn-out; he won't ever be as attractive as the suave charmer at your office. Your children have flown the coop and left you alone with your workaholic husband; they won't come back, not to stay. Your wife is a messy housekeeper and a lousy cook, she just doesn't think these things are important, even though they mean a lot to you; she probably isn't going to change.

Hope that things can change is not a blank check drawn on earthly perfection.

Coping with what is may be a realist's way of hoping for what can be.

An oyster cannot change the fact that a wee fleck, an irritating particle, has slipped inside its shell. So it accommodates. It finds a way to cope with what it cannot change. And by coping, the oyster creates an opalescent pearl. Not bad for mere coping.

Let me tell you the story of a man who discovered that he was not going to have the sensuous life of love that his heart told him he deserved.

In his head Larry never bought the illusion that he was born with an inalienable right to rapture. But in his *feelings*, he did; he really felt that he was cheated because he did not hear "Rhapsody in Blue" every time he made love.

He was not getting younger, something else he couldn't change, and he did not look agreeably on the thought that he was going to die without ever having slept with a beauty who would seduce him into love *fantastique*.

Larry blamed his fate on Corrie, pudgy, motherly Corrie, his wife, a woman not naturally equipped to turn married life into a sexual festival. He thought of leaving her to go in search of the love that would fulfill his life before it was forever too late. But he didn't have quite enough courage. Or he cared a little too much. He wasn't sure what it was that kept him.

He grew up a notch in the meantime, at age forty-five, and came to accept his life with its limits on fulfillment, and came at the same time to accept Corrie for the splendid, if limited, person she was. Having come this far, he also learned that he could do something himself about making their flat sex life a bit more bubbly. Which he did. And discovered, as the months went on, that life with Corrie could be comfortable, if not dazzling.

Bringing hope down to where we live, we get the power to accommodate ourself to the overcast skies of imperfect reality. Changing things that we can change. Accepting what we cannot change. And discovering that the things we cannot change are things with which we can live. This is hoping turned into coping.

We can discover that the story we are writing with our commitment is too good a story to put down before we finish it. We may remember the good parts in our private story and then start laughing at the rotten ones too. We may come to see that if we had thrown in the towel ten years ago, when we were on the ropes, life would not have been as good for either of us. So we settle for what we have, knowing that what we have is better than what we dared hope for back then. And that taken care of, we may figure there is nothing for it but to go to bed and see what happens next.

THERE IS LIFE AFTER COMMITMENT

When someone breaks an important commitment to us, we die, part of us dies anyway, a large part sometimes.

The good news is that there is life after the death of a commitment.

I don't mean to be facile about it, though. Living through the letdown that follows when someone tears up our life's commitment is a horror. To experience it is to die a minor death.

A minor death is the loss of one precious segment of our life, one that went a long way to make us who and what we are in this life. Sometimes when we die a minor death we feel as if we may as well be done with it, and die our major death too.

We experience our minor deaths as a walk through dark passages in a dark night. Each is a stage of death and dying. Let's listen, just for a moment, to the voices of people who remember groping their way through the long nights and sunless places.

Passage One. Anxiety.

"I felt that we trusted each other because we belonged to each other, and our trust gave me a stable footing. Now I am cut off, with nowhere to stand for sure. I have nothing to pin my life to, nothing to hook into, nothing to which I can secure myself. I feel as if I am floating unattached, unheld, unsupported—and the anxiety is killing me."

Passage Two. Loneliness.

"Nobody else can fill my emptiness. It is not the same as being alone; as long as I knew she was committed to me, I did not feel lonely even in solitude. Now my loneliness feels more like being lost, deserted, uncared for, unloved, unwanted. It is worse during those seasons we always celebrated with people we belonged to. Christmas is worst of all. Sometimes I have an urge to take every light and snuff it, every tree and burn it, every carol and silence it, so lonely is the time for me."

Passage Three. Unlovableness.

"I had love and I lost it. He knew me better than anyone on earth has ever known me, and he could not love me. Now I feel that if other people knew me as well as he did, they would all turn away from me. If he could not love me anymore, I must be unlovable."

Passage Four. Failure.

"I have failed at the one thing I needed most, wanted most, in all of life. Surely I could have done something to keep her. If only I had been a different person—better at love, more ready to praise, quicker to catch her moods—if only I had done more of this and less of that, I could have kept her. How bitter it is to be a failure at what matters most!"

Passage Five. Loss of identity.

"I *was* the person in our kitchen getting dinner for him. I *was* the person making love with him. I *was* the person who gave birth to our children. I *was* the person who tugged them through their childhoods. I *was* the person who plodded through the flat sides of our marriage with him. But who am I now? I cannot locate myself; he erased me when he left me. I am a missing person. And I would like to find myself before I die."

Dark passages, these are, all of them, leading through the minor death of a lost commitment.

Is there hope for life after the death of commitment?

Yes, there is hope. No guarantee. But honest hope. Realistic hope.

Maybe it is a hope that life can be fine without another lifetime commitment.

I received a letter yesterday from a woman named Phyllis. She recalled that after her divorce, she was floundering, lonely, and searching to find herself. She felt driven, she said, to find the perfect man for her. And then about a year ago, a light dawned inside of her and she realized that no man could bring her the happiness she sought—that what she needed was to grow within herself, alone. She learned that she had the capacity to enjoy anything and everything she wanted to, by herself, and that she did not need a man for this. Furthermore, she began to accept the fact that she was a worthy person and deserved a commitment from a man she trusted.

I remember Phyllis, and what I remember is a person alone in the dark passages, with little hope that life could be good again. But she waited. And waiting turned into a lively hope of being alive again, by herself, alone without loneliness.

The punchline of her letter, however, was that once she regained belief in herself, in life, in God, she was given the hope and the courage to make another commitment, if she had the chance. Well she did get the chance, and she took it.

Let me tell you about Irene too.

Irene came home one wretched day in May, found a note scribbled on a shopping memo stuck to the refrigerator door with a magnetic button. It was scrawled next to a reminder to pick up Clem's blue suit from the cleaner. The magnetic button had one of those mottoes meant to elevate common chores to the level of ministry: Divine Services Conducted Here Three Times Daily.

The note read, "l have left for Nevada with Hazel. I'll apply for a divorce there. Hazel and I are sure that this is God's will for us. I know that you will come to see it this way too. Will be in touch. Clem."

Irene plunked herself down on a kitchen chair, and conducted no divine services in the kitchen that day.

She had been Clem's devoted partner, dedicated to serving, though not to adoring, him, for twenty-two low church years. A professional-class soprano, she carried Clem's undisciplined baritone well enough for their duets to get regular billing on the sacred music circuit. But she also conducted divine services in the kitchen every Sunday, baking potatoes and meatloaf enough to feed the twenty-odd Christian soldiers who tooled in from the army base fifteen miles north of town to hear Clem preach his moral absolutes.

In any case, Clem's commitment to Irene had wilted before

the adoration which Hazel had become prone to offer him. He packed his bags, took off, and left Irene to walk her way alone through the dark passages of rejection.

She crawled through them with that homogenized blend of rage and shame we feel when someone we counted on lets us down. Rage at him for leaving her and shame that she did not have the stuff to make him stay. What hope was there for her now?

Hope? For a woman alone in the autumn shade of fifty? For a woman who had lived her life in the faith that a female's meaning was framed in service to a male? What hope?

Well, there was hope. It didn't come by waiting for it, as an illumination, the way it did for Phyllis. Irene created her own opportunities of hope.

She made new commitments to friends, and new kinds of commitments to her children. She kept her commitment to the people of her church, and took strength when they upped the ante on their commitment to her. But mostly she made new commitments to herself. She created a life more true to her real self than she had ever permitted herself in her wifely days.

She traveled, venturing to new and strange places with friends. Became a music teacher people competed to engage. She played games she had never played. Took risks she had never dared to take. And before too long she laughed again. Those of us who knew her before Clem ran off see a far more interesting person now, more fun to be with, more honest than she used to be while she served the Lord at Clem's side.

Maybe, in one cordoned-off section of her mind, she is actually grateful that Clem took off and left her. But if you were to ask her whether she would risk making another commitment to another man, she would probably say something like this: "Yes, to another kind of man, I would risk it again."

There is hope for life after the death of a commitment. We cannot feel it at the beginning; we cannot feel it while we pass through the passages of our minor death. But we can gradually open ourselves to it, be prepared to grasp it when it comes. And one way, one good way, to keep the door open to hope is by making and keeping commitments to other people, smaller, limited commitments to friends and neighbors, and a larger commitment to ourselves.

ONE DAY AT A TIME

Some people cannot sing the lyrics of promise to the tune of forever.

They need to commit themselves a day at a time.

A couple of people I know, we'll call them Jim and Pam, were on the ropes fifteen years ago, had lost hope, and figured they were finished. But they stumbled back together somehow, and admitted to each other that the word *forever* terrified them. So they committed themselves to each other again, not for an indefinite length of time, but for that day, to make it work that day, no more.

They celebrated their twentieth anniversary lately, and it looks for all the world as if they are together for keeps.

I asked Jim what the secret was, and this is what he told me.

"When we first got married we were dead serious about the 'for better or for worse' part, but the 'as long as life shall last' part had us scared from the beginning. We spent the first years of our marriage in graduate school, both of us into tough schedules up to our necks, and we got in each other's way a lot.

"When we had a fight about something, we would both wonder, Am I going to have put up with this the rest of my life? We saw years of fights rolling in on us from the future, and we knew we couldn't make it that long. We were intimidated by forever.

"When we decided to try again, we changed the terms of the commitment. We would not talk about forever. We would not even think about forever. We would make unreserved commitments for today.

"We were relieved to shed the burden of forever. And we were more relaxed about the painful things that happened between us. They did not scare us anymore because we stopped imagining a lifetime of them. Day by day was easier.

"Our commitment is as real and deep as ever. We just don't stretch it across the years ahead."

All of us who make a lifetime commitment wonder sometimes, when troubles come, whether we can keep it all the years ahead. Especially when we look bad things straight in the eye and admit they are not going to change. The desire to make commitment last forever gets crippled by fear. But we can cope creatively with each other today. So why not keep our eyes on the *now* of a commitment, and let the forever take care of itself?

"Tomorrow, tomorrow, I love you, tomorrow. You're always a day away." Little Orphan Annie's song was a Broadway version of Jesus' wisdom: "Be not anxious about tomorrow. Sufficient unto the day is the trouble thereof."

I am not prescribing for everyone. A lot of us can handle the lifetime prospect. But people who are intimidated by the thought of forever may find that committing by the day is the best way to create fidelity for life.

IS GOD COMMITTED?

Ultimately, the question of hope gets us to the question of God, and of whether he is committed to us. Will God *be there* for us? Does he personally care enough to keep a commitment to people who wonder what the odds of making it are?

No matter what our faith or doubt or disbelief may be, the ultimate question is whether God is committed to us.

My fascination with the question of whether God is really up there cools down quickly if I cannot believe he is committed to me down here, and to others, to weak, needy, faulty people like me. But in those moments when the current of his committed presence flows into my weakness, his reality becomes ultimately important to me.

When I feel that I am committed to, unconditionally, I sense that God's being has become transparent to me. I know what I want to know most about who he is and what he has in mind. And I get new hope for my own commitments to other people.

I get reassurance from stories of other people's experiences that tell them he is committed to them in spite of everything. And it helps to know that people with a lot more faith than I have sometimes wondered whether they can depend on God's commitment. Biblical stories are often the best. Take the one about Moses and his surprising experience with the burning bush.

God had been on leave of absence for four hundred years— as far as anybody could tell—and four hundred years is a long time for anyone to be away. Even for God. People forget someone who stays away too long. And, as a matter of fact, Moses didn't even know God's name.

Moses, who had been brought up in the Egyptian Pharaoh's court, was living in exile at the time, a fugitive from Pharaoh—and, for that matter, from his own people—when God spotted him alone in the wilderness tending his father-in-law's sheep. God flagged him down with a burning piece of chaparral that flamed oddly long. Moses went to take a second look, out of mere curiosity, but it was not what he saw, it was what he heard there that shifted the winds of the future. God had come back.

The Lord was committed to renewing his relationship with the human family, and he wanted Moses to go back to Egypt, where the Hebrews had been slaves for four centuries, and prepare them for escape into freedom and a new commitment to God.

Moses had reservations. Who wouldn't? It would be very hard to feel at ease with a God who stayed away that long from people who needed his help as much as those Hebrew slaves needed it. Who was this unseen presence, this awesome voice, and the stranger behind the voice? Moses needed a name for this presence.

For an ancient Jew, to ask somebody's name was really to ask for a hint of his personal character. So when Moses asked for God's name, he was asking, "What sort of God are you?" God obliged. He told Moses his name.

The name told Moses what he wanted to know. Enough, anyway, for him to go back to Egypt and lead his people out of bondage.

What was that name? Moses knew. But it is not easy to say now. The Jewish people came to consider the name too holy for any ordinary person to put on human tongue. And with a divine name, like most things, we lose it if we don't use it. What was written in the Torah was only four consonants, YHWH, no vowels. And who could even pronounce a word without vowels, let alone know what it meant?

When the ancient Jews spoke of this God, they simply substituted another name for the original, so they always knew what they were doing. But when it came to putting the Hebrew name into English, we had a problem. The educated guess was that it was originally a form of the verb *to be*. So it got translated as something like "I am who I am." which seemed to convey a deep philosophical truth about divine essence and divine existence.

But Moses was not a philosopher, and what he really wanted to know was whether the stranger could be trusted. Would he be there when a God was really needed? Moses did not really care, at that moment, about God's essence; he cared about his presence.

So probably YHWH, the name God gave him at the burning bush, comes across best in English something like this: *"the one who will be there with you, the God who has made a commitment to you and intends to keep it."*

No one could have guessed then the fantastic story that was going to follow this strange encounter in the desert. One crisis after another. And whenever crises came, people always asked the same question: "Is the Lord here with us?" If they knew God was keeping his commitment, they received strength to keep theirs. When it looked as if God was not keeping his commitment, they lost hope for their own commitments.

What I want to know about God is exactly what Moses wanted to know. Is he committed to me? If I can't keep my commitments to other people, is God still committed to me? To his human family? To the world?

When I do feel that he is the God who will be there—in the worst as well as the best of places—I feel that keeping personal commitments is what holds life together for me and gives it a future. And I get my confidence back. Commitment *is* what makes any human sort of life together possible on this earth.

It isn't that commitments suddenly get easy to keep when we believe God is committed to us. I've not had much experience, personally, with miracle solutions to the problems and pains that make keeping commitments hard sometimes—though if miracles work for you, be thankful for them. But when I feel that God is keeping his commitment to me, to us, to the world, in spite of a lot of reasons we've given him for calling it quits with us, it makes more sense for me to keep commitments I make to other people.

I am not a hopeful person by nature. When things get tough I am easily tempted to believe that the jig is up. I foreclose on the future all too soon. If my team is not ahead by at least two touchdowns in the final five minutes of play, I hear defeat blowing in the winds. In my marriage I have often had to be rescued from my own pessimism by Doris's power to hope that there were good possibilities within the worst of our problems. I sometimes suspected that she was denying reality. But she was not denying; she really saw possibilities to which my despair had blinded me.

Out of my private struggles with despair, I have come to see that hope is the final secret of all commitment.

When two people are committed to each other, when the innerspring of their commitment is care, each for the other, there are possibilities in the toughest situations. Not certainties. But possibilities. Not possibilities of things being all we've ever wanted them to be. But possibilities of things becoming better than they are. Good enough to make the future together, as friends, as partners, as family, better for having kept on caring for each other just a little more than we care for ourselves.

In sum, what I've been saying here is that commitments live on hope. Not on duty, not on what we are obligated to do, but on hope for what we can do. And for what others can do for us. Hope is the alternative to the seductions of the uncommitted life.

Hope is energy.

Hope is energy to cope when life gets tough. And, when you get down to brass tacks, it is the energy we need for commitment keeping in a world where somebody, at any moment, may rain on your parade.

CHAPTER 13

Taking Charge of Our Future

We possess two powers to create a future worth living in. One of them is the power to forgive. The other is the power to make and keep commitments. We can use them both to secure a future for our most precious relationships.

The power to forgive frees us from past pains that we cannot accept and cannot forget.

When we forgive, we ignore the normal laws that strap us to our painful pasts. We fly over a dues-paying morality in order to create a new future out of the past's unfairness. When we forgive other people, especially people to whom we are committed, we untie ourselves from the unfair pain they caused us. When we forgive ourselves, we unshackle ourselves from unfair pain that we inflicted on others. We thaw a past that was frozen in pain, and shake ourselves free to face the future.

Just as the power of forgiveness releases us from a painful past, the power to make promises creates a foundation for a hopeful future.

"The remedy for the . . . chaotic uncertainty of the future is contained in the faculty to make and keep promises." Hannah Arendt wrote this at the conclusion of her epochal book *The Human Condition*. With commitments, she said, we create "islands of security" within a wild sea of insecurities. This is the power of commitment—the ability to secure our vital personal relationships against the tides of disillusionment.

Commitment is our unique human power to stand up against the whims of fate and circumstance. It ranks alongside of, maybe even above, the other noble faculties that civilized human beings applaud themselves for having—intelligence, great feeling, and imagination. "How noble in reason! How infinite in faculty! . . . in apprehension how like a god!" Let Shakespeare go on about our likeness to a rational divinity. The truth is that none of us is ever more God-like than when we simply make and simply keep commitments to each other.

There is much about our future that is out of our hands. We are stuck with the genes we neither earned nor asked for. We are sucked into the deadly games played by principalities and powers of this world. We are walloped by private tragedies and gifted by divine providence. And we all rise and fall with the American dollar. Yes, some things *are* beyond our control.

But we have control over the most important arena where we live out our lives: we can decide, once, and then a thousand times over, that we will keep our caring commitments to people. This power, when we choose to use it, is what breathes lasting life into the most precious facet of our future, the relationships we have with people we love.

It is a paradox. For we use power to limit our power—to tie ourself to a promise, a promise we made once, a year ago, a life-time ago, a promise we intended then to keep. And we give someone else the right to hold us to that promise. All of which sounds more like losing control than taking control, like being stuck with the past more than taking charge of the future.

But that is the paradox! Being bound to a promise we make is only a way to set the stage for a future that is in our hands.

The promise we made yesterday is like the foundation an architect lays for the building he is planning. Once he has the foundation, he is free to improvise, to change, to recreate all the rooms in his building. He is free to improve on his plans as he goes. But he needs the foundation to make it possible.

It's that way with commitments. The promise we make at the beginning is the foundation. From then on we are on our own to write the story of our relationship with another person. The foundation only gives us a continuing chance to keep on creating our future.

Each moment is a new beginning. In every decision we swipe the Fates aside and take charge of our future with another person. We change our mind, we improvise, we adjust, we suffer, we wait, we forgive, we move in and out of love, and we accommodate ourself to the shifting scenes of our life as we move from stage to stage on our journey. And we can make all our moves, freely, on the foundation we created by our commitment.

Life does not always feel as if we are in charge of it. Whenever a lasting relationship goes sour, we can feel fated, checkmated by things we cannot control. We feel bound by our obsessions. We feel driven by unsatisfied desires. We feel crippled by whacky parents. We feel stuck in a miserable or, at best, boring marriage. We feel trapped in an illicit love affair. And disabled by diverse demons tangled in the dark grottos of our soul. All in all, we do not always feel like a giant in charge of our future. We feel more like an eagle with clipped wings and cuffed legs.

We shop for a therapist who can work a magic that we cannot perform alone. But the therapist can only help us take responsibility for ourselves and take control of our own future.

In her book *Married People*, Francine Klagsbrun remarks that "People who stay happily married see themselves not as victims, but as free agents who make choices in life." This is the key. The first choice we make about our future is about ourselves. Are we victims or are we choosers? The initial, and the most critical, choice in commitments is the choice to say no to the victim syndrome and yes to the power of keeping promises.

Of course if another person always met all of our needs, we could glide through the future with him or her without even thinking about commitment. If the flame of desire for the other person never flickered, we would never feel pressured by a promise we made when we didn't know what keeping it would cost.

But most of us keep our commitments in spite of at least some good or bad reasons for not keeping them. Commitment was invented precisely because of the "in spite of" that haunts every lasting relationship. No matter when or where we live, we keep our commitments in spite of two factors that are present in every close human association.

First, we suffer a global epidemic of imperfection. It hits people of every race, every culture, every faith. Every relationship is carried on imperfectly by imperfect people. Every friend is flawed. Every spouse has failings. Every son or daughter is faulty. Every commitment ever made, this side of Eden, has been made by a flawed person to a flawed person. So we always keep our commitments in spite of the imperfections of the people to whom we make them.

Second, each of us is unique, different from every other. Inside or outside, we are all, at certain points, strangers to each other. Which is the way it should be, because our mysteries make us interesting. Besides, if you are different from me you offer me something I cannot find in myself.

But differences can push us apart too; if other people are too different from us, they do not attract us, they threaten us. If you have too many habits that look crazy to me, if you use too many words I cannot understand, if you have too many beliefs that are alien to mine, if your quirks are too strange, I am likely to withdraw from you, and look for someone a little more like me. Our differences can become our incompatibility.

So we are imperfect and we are different. And we keep our commitments in spite of it. In fact, commitments are all about staying together in spite of our imperfections and our differences. Somehow love has to be kept alive, for no real relationship lasts unless love lasts. The shell can survive, but the relationship dies for lack of love. And the only love that lasts is the promised love of commitment.

Relationships do not die because the whimsical gods of eros stop smiling on us. Nor do they survive because the gods of eros fan the flame of our desire. Our romantic feelings float with the Fates; erotic love flickers and fades, flourishes and flounders. But lasting relationships do not depend on the fickle Fates or changeable gods of eros.

We decide for ourself whether we will keep the promises of love. Not fate, not destiny, not accident, but our own choices keep our pivotal personal relationships going.

Remember that every genuine personal commitment has two components: consistency and care.

Consistency keeps the external structure steady. But care breathes lasting love inside the structure. Consistency is the backbone; care is the heart. Consistency is the muscle; care is the warm blood. Consistency is our predictability; care is our personal presence.

We are consistent to the extent that we choose to be. An obvious point. But caring too is a matter of choice. We do not fall into care. Not the way we fall in love.

We have to choose to care. At least to care enough to respect the other person as a duly accredited image of God, not to be coerced, deceived, or demeaned. We have to choose to encourage the other person to develop and deploy his or her own gifts—even if they compete with ours, to honor the other person's trust, to accommodate ourself to unsatisfactory realities within our relationship, to applaud the other person when she dances to the tempo of her own music. We have to choose to care.

We put caring love into motion; care is at least as much action as feeling. We don't *feel* caringly, and then expect the other person to be grateful for the care we feel. We do things, specific things, that give flesh and blood to the feelings we have when we care for someone.

The nuts and bolts of caring are sometimes dictated by tragedy. For James Ettison, it was Alice's tragic accident. For Eric Zorg, it was Karen's Alzheimer's disease. Jim and Eric had their choices made for them by every hour's new needs. And we will have our hours when caring takes on a form we did not choose.

But we also create our own landscapes of care, patterns of care. Call them *carescapes*. The design of lived-out commitment. Here are some samplers.

We listen. Listening is the silent shape of caring. We listen to what the other person says to us. But we listen closest when no words are spoken. We listen for the unuttered message of feeling. We listen for pain expressed in disguised sighs. We listen for desires heard only in the language of the eyes. We listen to our own messages to learn how they were heard through the filter of the other person's needs. Listening is a large part of our carescapes.

We stay awake. A caring person stays alert to what is happening. We notice the little things that have large meaning. We keep our wits about us when a trifling temptation at five o'clock in the afternoon could take us where we don't want to be at ten in the evening. We don't sleep through the storm signals that the other person is waving in front of us. I wonder how many relationships flounder because one person is too fuzzy-headed to see what is going on when the drug of desire deadens his sense for another person's needs.

We stay in tune with reality. Caring takes the form of accommodation to things we cannot change. We accommodate to the failings of another person. We choose not to live by fantasies of the ideal friend, the perfectly satisfying spouse, the superior child. We create our carescapes on the estate of human imperfection.

We forgive. Caring on the longer journey takes shape in forgiveness. We can, if we choose, always go for the jugular, getting at least an eye for an eye and, if possible, two of theirs for one of ours. Or we can choose the way of healing for the wounds of unfair injury.

Our carescapes are nurseries of healing for the hurts we want to go away in relationships we want to keep. Forgiving is the healing art. It is the one way to make new beginnings at the painful point of where we are—not where we wish we were, but where we are, in pain, with the only person to whom we are coupled. The carescapes of promised love are watered with forgiveness.

We stay honest. Caring is nurtured in the truth. And honesty comes whole, not piecemeal; we have to *be* truthful if we hope to *speak* truthfully. So if we care for another person, we will be our very self, not a fake, not a masked self, in her presence. We will credit the other person with maturity enough to cope with our truth. And we will ask for truth in turn. Our carescapes go to seed if we do not plant them in truthfulness.

These are a few of the visible and touchable shapes in our landscapes of caring. In our carescapes.

So we come back to the center of this last, brief chapter: in the keeping of commitments, we take charge of the future by sustaining the personal relationships that make our life most worth living.

Of course we have to keep some doors open for retreat from bad commitments. The opening words of this book give witness. I said there that life would be a mess if all we could get from each other was, "I'll be there if I can, but don't count on it." But I also said that life would be cruel if we were absolutely stuck to every commitment we made.

Slavery to every commitment we make is a fanatical caricature of commitment. Some commitments are terrible mistakes. We

CHRISTIAN HERALD
People Making A Difference

Christian Herald is a family of dedicated, Christ-centered ministries that reaches out to deprived children in need, and to homeless men who are lost in alcoholism and drug addiction. Christian Herald also offers the finest in family and evangelical literature through its book clubs and publishes a popular, dynamic magazine for today's Christians.

Our Ministries

Family Bookshelf and **Christian Bookshelf** provide a wide selection of inspirational reading and Christian literature written by best-selling authors. All books are recommended by an Advisory Board of distinguished writers and editors.

Christian Herald magazine is contemporary, a dynamic publication that addresses the vital concerns of today's Christian. Each monthly issue contains a sharing of true personal stories written by people who have found in Christ the strength to make a difference in the world around them.

Christian Herald Children. The door of God's grace opens wide to give impoverished youngsters a breath of fresh air, away from the evils of the streets. Every summer, hundreds of youngsters are welcomed at the Christian Herald Mont Lawn Camp located in the Poconos at Bushkill, Pennsylvania. Year-round assistance is also provided, including teen programs, tutoring in reading and writing, family counseling, career guidance and college scholarship programs.

The Bowery Mission. Located in New York City, the Bowery Mission offers hope and Gospel strength to the downtrodden and homeless. Here, the men of Skid Row are fed, clothed, ministered to. Many voluntarily enter a 6-month discipleship program of spiritual guidance, nutrition therapy and Bible study.

Our Father's House. Located in rural Pennsylvania, Our Father's House is a discipleship and job training center. Alcoholics and drug addicts are given an opportunity to recover, away from the temptations of city streets.

Christian Herald ministries, founded in 1878, are supported by the voluntary contributions of individuals and by legacies and bequests. Contributions are tax deductible. Checks should be made out to Christian Herald Children, The Bowery Mission, or to Christian Herald Association.

Administrative Office: 40 Overlook Drive, Chappaqua, New York 10514
Telephone: (914) 769-9000

 Fully-accredited Member
of the Evangelical Council
for Financial Accountability

make commitments that we cannot keep. And commitments we should not keep.

But the final truth about us—the truth that matters most—is our power to keep our human relationships alive, our power to make and keep commitments. If we trade in this power for the quick fixes of the uncommitted life, we threaten our own future. Hell is a forever without commitment. We cannot survive, cannot preserve our humanity, without enduring relationships of caring love.

Human fellowship and sturdy joy come to us as we create and keep on recreating our fragile human relationships, making them last through the power of caring love. To dare to make and care to keep commitments—this is to live. To live the life of promised love.